W9-BQT-226

MAR - - 2007

306 .8742 DIA
Diamond, Michael J.,
My father before me :
72871279

145

WHITE RIVER BRANCH

Johnson County Public Library
401 State Street
Franklin, IN 46131

WITHDRAWN

3-13-07

MY FATHER BEFORE ME

ALSO BY MICHAEL J. DIAMOND

*Becoming a Father: Contemporary Social,
Developmental, and Clinical Perspectives*

(COEDITOR, WITH JERROLD L. SHAPIRO, PHD,
AND MARTIN GREENBERG, MD)

WHITE RIVER BRANCH
1664 LIBRARY BLVD.
GREENWOOD, IN 46162

MY FATHER BEFORE ME

*How Fathers and Sons
Influence Each Other
Throughout Their Lives*

MICHAEL J. DIAMOND

W. W. Norton & Company • New York • London

All of the individuals that I discuss in this book are drawn from my clinical practice and personal experience. With the exception of my immediate family, all names, most places, and many identifying characteristics have been changed in the interest of protecting the privacy and anonymity of the individuals referred to.

Copyright © 2007 by Michael J. Diamond

All rights reserved
Printed in the United States of America
First Edition

For information about permission to reproduce selections from this book, write to Permissions, W. W. Norton & Company, Inc., 500 Fifth Avenue, New York, NY 10110

Manufacturing by Courier Westford
Book design by Iris Weinstein
Production manager: Anna Oler

Library of Congress Cataloging-in-Publication Data
Diamond, Michael J., 1944–
My father before me : how fathers and sons influence
each other throughout their lives /
Michael J. Diamond. — 1st ed.
p. cm.
Includes bibliographical references and index.
ISBN-13: 978-0-393-06060-7 (hardcover)
ISBN-10: 0-393-06060-8 (hardcover)
1. Fathers and sons. 2. Fatherhood. I. Title.
HQ755.85.D53 2007
306.874'2—dc22
2006033195

W. W. Norton & Company, Inc.
500 Fifth Avenue, New York, N.Y. 10110
www.wwnorton.com

W. W. Norton & Company Ltd.
Castle House, 75/76 Wells Street, London W1T 3QT

1 2 3 4 5 6 7 8 9 0

To my treasured family who enliven my life in infinite ways:
My wife Linda, and our children, Maya and Alex

And in loving memory of my parents,
Moe and Elaine Diamond

I enjoy talking to very old men, for they have gone before us, as it were, on a road that we too must probably tread, and it seems to me that we can find out from them what it is like and whether it is rough and difficult or broad and easy.

—SOCRATES in Plato's *Republic*[1]

CONTENTS

ACKNOWLEDGMENTS

The seeds of this book have been germinating in my mind for many years as I grappled with my own understanding of fathering, men and masculinity, and the many facets of being both son and father.

I am deeply grateful to my dear friend and colleague Jerry Shapiro, a fellow traveler himself for the last three decades, with whom I have intimately shared so many of the feelings, thoughts, and ideas that culminated in *My Father Before Me*. Jerry generously offered invaluable editorial suggestions and encouragement as well as informed advice on the subject of writing for a wider audience. Several close psychoanalytic colleagues and friends, particularly Steven Axelrod, Dianne Elise, Alan Spivak, Peter Wolson, and Harriet Wrye, provided inspiration, illumination, and encouragement of my nascent ideas through years of rich dialogue, and consequently, helped me to refine my own thinking. And most significantly, my appreciation is immeasurable for my wife and closest friend, Linda, who supported my work on this project in inestimable ways, including a thorough and critical reading of the manuscript in process, while challenging me as only a highly trusted and loving partner can do.

I am thankful to so many of my colleagues with the Los Angeles Institute and Society for Psychoanalytic Studies—students and supervisees; teachers and mentors; friends, allies, and rivals—all of whom have enlivened my continuing journey along the road toward a deeper understanding of the complexities of being human. I would be remiss if I didn't express my gratitude to the "forefathers" of my psychological literacy, particularly two Stanford University graduate school mentors, Philip Zimbardo and the late Ernest R. Hilgard. Furthermore, numerous psychoanalytic scholars have profoundly influenced my own work on fathering and masculine development—in particular, the writings of many contemporary psychoanalytic thinkers, including Jessica Benjamin, Peter Blos, Calvin Colarusso, Irene Fast, James Herzog, William Pollack, Kyle Pruett, and John Munder Ross.

I am especially indebted to *Los Hombres Sinceros*—Saul Brown, Dan Minton, Robert Moradi, and Bob Tzudiker—for the wisdom, playfulness, trust, and authenticity that we've shared together over the last fifteen years. In addition, several others helped to foster this book without realizing it. Alan Holtzman encouraged me to extrapolate from my professional writings and carve out something that might directly reach fathers, mothers, and sons; the late Jeff Beane promoted a deeper understanding of the issues that gay men face; Marty Greenberg (with whom I had coedited a text ten years ago) assisted me in finding a language that conveys the incomparable experience of becoming a father; and Barry Miller helped me to create an internal space where my own muse could thrive.

I wish also to thank my editor at W. W. Norton, Maria Guarnaschelli, who grasped what was unique in my thinking, and whose perspicacity and creative editorial guidance helped to make this book one that could make a difference in the lives of its readers. In addition, I am thankful for the thoughtful professionalism provided by Norton's Emma Dumain, Robin Muller, Sarah Rothbard, and Katrina Washington. My agent, Lynn Seligman, recognized the value of this project many years ago and worked to help it to become a reality; her perseverance is appreciated. And I am grateful to Roberta Israeloff—a writer and mother of two boys herself—who "felt" my ideas and worked closely with me in the writing process to elaborate upon my clinical and personal experience in order to establish the frame for communicating as broadly as I would hope.

There are many others who cannot be thanked by name: the patients, supervisees, acquaintances, strangers, and friends whose experiences led to my own understandings and whose privacy I am committed to protect by taking steps to preserve their anonymity. Without these individuals, there would be no *My Father Before Me*.

Finally, and most especially, I want to express my deepest appreciation to my children, Maya and Alex; and to my father, the late Moe Diamond, who placed his love for his children at the center of his life, inspiring me to do the same. Largely thanks to his legacy, I can allow my children to remind me that love in itself is not enough, but rather must be continually leavened with understanding, authority, humility, patience, hard work, and the courage to bear not knowing.

MY FATHER BEFORE ME

INTRODUCTION

Until I was seventeen years old, I played organized youth baseball. By that time, most of the other kids' fathers who had regularly attended the games stopped coming—the guys no longer felt it was "cool" for fathers to show up. I knew that my father, who taught me to love baseball, wanted nothing more than to sit in the bleachers and watch me play. But needing to feel more independent of my family, I insisted that he stay home. I could not bear the embarrassment of knowing he was there. It seemed as if his very presence made me appear less mature.

One afternoon, I came home after a particularly exciting game, and my dad asked me how things had gone. "Pretty good," I said, in typical laconic teenage fashion.

"I heard you doubled in a run," he said.

"How did you know about my double?" I asked, suddenly suspicious. Visibly flustered, he stammered something about running into one of the coaches, but I knew he was lying.

"I saw the game," he finally confessed.

"How?" I demanded. The crowd has been sparse that day, and I knew that he could not have been in the stands.

"There's a gap in the bushes behind the fence in left field," he said. "You can't see me, but I can watch the game."

His confession stunned me, but I was feeling more than just stunned at that moment—I was angry, furious even, betrayed by his intrusion. How dare he violate my privacy and spy on me! At the same time, I had to admit that a part of me was secretly pleased that he had witnessed my performance, and grateful that he had found a way to accomplish this without my knowing, even if the thought of his sneaking around made me uneasy.

These turbulent and confusing emotions were simply too much for me to make sense of, much less sort out. And so I did what most teenage boys do in this situation: I shut down.

It was not until I was the father of a teenage son myself that I could more fully understand how conflicted my father must have been, having to weigh his wish to honor my request against his own desire to watch his son do something we both loved so much. Only because I have experienced these conflicting desires with my own son, who has busily drawn his boundaries around what he will and will not share with me, can I now fully appreciate my father and deeply admire him, particularly for his loving efforts to respect my wishes while simultaneously sharing in my accomplishments.

I only wish that he were still alive so that I could tell him this. I'd also love to ask him a question: "How did you do it?" What I want to know is how he was able to recognize and respect my teenage need to separate myself from the family while still understanding that I wanted very much to be a part of it. And at the same time, how did he so easily seem to appreciate that I craved and valued his pride and respect as much as I did my privacy and independence?

Today, I am not only a father but also a psychoanalyst. I have studied human development extensively and witnessed its manifestation in my clinical practice with patients, as well as at home where I've watched my own children grow. At long last I realize that my own father was able to identify with my contradictory needs—to be independent and to be connected—because he experienced the same conflict when he was a boy himself. I am certain that, just as for myself, both needs existed within him, butting heads, and neither one canceled out the other. Recognizing his own internal conflict allowed him to become the kind of father who, at least on this occasion, could endure my anger and disappointment. He knew that I was angry with him, that I wanted to reject him, but he did not take it personally, and because of this, he did not feel the need to retaliate or become withdrawn or depressed himself. Instead, he maintained his fatherly presence, which in turn inspired me to provide the same sort of a model for my own son when I became a father myself.

This chain of complex interactions, exchange of feelings, desire to both identify and differentiate, and the sense of looking back to understand one's father while looking ahead to envision the life of one's son, constitute the crux of the father-son relationship.

Despite the apparent timelessness of the father-son bond— and more generally, the father-child connection—a sense of its power and closeness has waxed and waned over time. In agrarian society, for instance, fathers were very involved in their children's lives, acting as teachers, mentors, and guides. This involvement began to ebb in the mid-nineteenth century with the advent of the Industrial Revolution. As families moved from the farm to the city, men began working outside of the home, and as a consequence, their home-centered influence decreased. By the end of World War II, fathers were seldom thought of as contributing to their children's healthy development. Instead, they were more notable for their absence, or for their destructive impact, as when they were abusive, neglectful, or dead. In many ways, the successful father had become the forgotten parent.[1]

Effective fathers were not only absent from the popular imagination but from the professional literature as well. Scholarly papers documenting mothers, motherhood, and a mother's impact on her children abounded; social scientists unwittingly devalued the father's role, and research on fathers was scant. Even now, when we talk about fatherhood, we tend to focus on its concrete trappings: the diapers men change, the parent-teacher conferences they attend, the soccer games they coach, the custody battles they win. Meanwhile, important questions go unanswered. How does becoming a father change a man, and in what ways? What is the impact of becoming a father on a man's partner? How does his becoming a father affect a man's relationship to his own father? How do fathers and sons feel about each other? The emotions that coincide with being a father—emotions such as hope and fear, joy and pain—have until now remained largely unexplored.

When dads did appear in literary and psychological contexts, their *symbolic* presence was emphasized while they were taken to have no real positive influence on their children's development. But their actual presence—the rich and profound ways that fathers can and do influence their children's lives—was neglected. This neglect of the father's positive impact on the lives of his children leads to many unhappy consequences. They include buttressing our society's tendency to minimize a father's crucially active contribution, and holding mothers entirely accountable for their children's development while exonerating fathers except when they are notably destructive.

Our tendency to ignore or discount a father's influence began to change in the 1970s for several reasons. With the first stirrings of the women's rights movement and an outpouring of feminist theory, huge social upheavals ensued. As women flocked to join the workforce and families adapted to support dual careers, men had to become more active parents, causing gender roles to become more flexible. At the same time, changes in obstetrical and pediatric practices enabled fathers to become more directly involved in pregnancy, delivery, and pediatric care. Lamaze natural childbirth classes, for example, which became very popular during this era, welcomed fathers as pregnancy coaches, and trained them to assist during birth as well. Finally, thanks to advances in the techniques of behavioral and psycho-physiological observation, researchers studying infants began to examine the importance of the father-child bond.

Today, we recognize that fathers have a unique and essential role to play in raising children. A father does not merely supplement what a mother does but complements her role. He has an important impact on his child deriving from his fatherliness, from the fact that he is a man, extending from the day of conception, beyond his own death, until the day his child dies. Even fatherless children feel the impact of their fathers; that is, they create an internalized, paternal image based on fact, fantasy, and familial and cultural folklore, which influences them throughout their lives.

This much is common knowledge, at least among professionals working with this population. Less acknowledged is the other half of the equation, the fact that just as profoundly as fathers influence their sons, so do sons influence their fathers. This is not to say that fathers don't have a significant influence on their daughters and vice versa: they do. But because of various biological, cultural, and psychological factors, the relationship between fathers and sons is particularly intricate and complex. Their unique bond naturally emerges from each one's ease of identifying with the other's maleness, from their fundamental biological resemblance. Because of this intense *mutual identification*, they each have an especially multifaceted impact upon one another throughout the course of their lives.

My research has shown that while traversing certain developmental milestones—moving from infancy to toddlerhood, childhood to adolescence, or younger adulthood to midlife—father and son interact in the developmental crucible. They strongly impact one another in a multitude of ways. In the intertwined father-son relationship, these influences are reciprocal. Each experiences the impact of the other. Optimally, each grows and develops in step with the other.

According to this understanding, becoming a father, one of life's most important challenges, is more than a watershed event in a man's life. It is a complex interaction during which the father influences the way his child develops, and, simultaneously, his son affects the way that his father handles his own parallel transitions. At any given moment, fathers and sons are working through their own issues, yet they are also uniquely positioned to help each other grow and take the next step.

Throughout this book, as I discuss the roles that fathers assume in order to help their sons grow, I will simultaneously describe how fathers themselves are launched on a process of growth that parallels their sons' journeys. I follow fathers and sons through the life cycle as they work together and struggle against one another. In examining the complexities of this singular relationship, I pay particular attention to the internal, primarily emotional experiences of both father and son as they influence each other through a wide range of circumstances.[2]

Dividing a human life into phases is always arbitrary. Any listing of markers and milestones is limited in that it is theoretical and people aren't: they are living and breathing human beings whose trajectories couldn't be more idiosyncratic. Still, to begin a conversation about the ways in which fathers and sons influence each other, I need to generalize about certain roles and time periods. Thus, for example, to become guardians of infants, fathers assume a new set of responsibilities and are challenged to redefine their sense of masculinity. As a liaison for their sons' entry to the larger world, men learn to appreciate "otherness," that is, to recognize that other people have an existence apart from theirs, which is the root of empathy. When boys need their fathers to become models and to approve of their behavior, men are called upon to develop their sense of paternal authority and personal responsibility. As boys contend with the "oedipal stage," their fathers confront, contain, and more appropriately express their own difficult emotions, particularly aggression, envy, jealousy, and competitiveness. For their elementary school–aged sons who need guidance, fathers are asked to develop the ability to teach and guide. Fathers of teenage boys learn to ride the roller coaster—to maintain their emotional equilibrium, to modulate their vulnerability—in the face of their sons' adulation and subsequent devaluation. As boys turn into young men, fathers begin to learn the lessons of "letting go" and surrendering their authority—a significant loss—to their sons' burgeoning autonomy. As the father of adult sons, fathers learn to confront their own dependency needs, and to find ways to leave a legacy that will survive their own death as mentors to their grandchildren and future generations. Finally, fathers learn to face and accept their own death, frequently through the help of their older sons.

Throughout this process, as fathers actively parent their sons, they also have the opportunity to reconcile with and resolve unfinished business with their own fathers and mothers. Moreover, by becoming and staying involved in fathering, men undergo emotional, psychological, moral, and even physical changes. According to the psychiatrist and author Kyle Pruett, engaged fathers tend to be more emotionally available, more open-minded and flexible, and healthier.[3] They also live longer. Indeed, the impact that father and child have upon one another will only become more apparent and profound as the years elapse.

To write this book, I drew on my more than thirty years' experience as a practicing psychotherapist, couples therapist, and psychoanalyst with specialized work in the father-son relationship. The text is based on my clinical observations and research findings, reinforced by case histories from my practice, that began over two decades ago when I initially examined the hopes and dreams as well as the anxieties and needs of men in the process of becoming fathers. A few years later, I studied how fathering helps men to establish their sense of manhood. Shortly thereafter, my investigations turned toward understanding the specific impact of fathers on their sons throughout their life span and, in turn, how a son influences his father's own parallel development. Most recently, my research has focused on how fathers help to shape their sons' flexible and healthy sense of masculinity and how this masculine identity shifts during the course of a man's life.[4]

My exploration of the benefits and vicissitudes of the father-son relationship, and my discussion of gender and what it means be a "man," are derived from a new vision of masculinity that has only recently made its debut in the mainstream discourse on gender and sexuality in America. Writing about the male gender, it's easy to fall into one of two camps: to view masculinity as either biologically determined, transmitted through evolution and therefore unchangeable; or as a social construct, environmentally and culturally created, and as such infinitely change-able. My goal is to avoid this polarity in order to navigate between them, to eschew "either/or" thinking in favor of an outlook that encompasses "both/and."

In our culture, it is not enough to be a man biologically. Masculinity has to be proven over and over again. Essentially, the most important thing about being a man comes down to the fact that a man is not a woman. In this light, masculinity has become a zero-sum game: a male can claim to be masculine only by completely renouncing femininity. Therefore, the broader and more flexible sense of masculinity espoused in this book is rooted in the understanding that men need to acknowledge and accept all aspects of themselves, including those that society identifies as "feminine," as inherent components of their masculinity.

It's important to note that I am not arguing simply for a "kinder and gentler" masculinity; a man doesn't have to acknowledge his femininity by strapping milk bottles to his chest and pretending he's breast-feeding a baby. But neither does he need to strut around with an assault rifle slung over his shoulder or display bulging biceps to prove he's King of the Hill. Rather, this new view of masculinity sustains the paradoxical interior realities of a man's experience that both masculinity and femininity commingle throughout his life.

My insights are derived from varied sources, such as listening to my patients during my years of work as a psychoanalyst and therapist; from dialogues and conversations with other psychoanalytic colleagues and researchers in the field; through assumptions drawn from studying the work of such major contributors as Freud and Winnicott as well as more contemporary scholars investigating fathering and male development; and from my observations of fathers and sons interacting in the world around me. This includes conversations with men I met on class trips and at ball fields—men from across the socioeconomic spectrum, many of whom would never have found their way to a therapist's office. Finally, this book reflects my own hard-won understanding and painstaking analysis of my experiences as a son, father, and husband.

The understanding of the unique bond between fathers and sons is still evolving. As it does, my hope is that this book will contribute to knowledge slowly being accumulated and expanded upon, and will also inspire the men who read it to approach their roles as fathers with seriousness and purposefulness.[5] In truth, they are heeding the call to a new kind of internal journey, one that they will undertake alongside their sons for the betterment of both, a journey toward the realization of William Wordsworth's wise counsel that ultimately "The Child is father of the Man."[6]

I

FATHERHOOD ON THE HORIZON

Your son is at five your master,
at ten your servant,
at fifteen your double,
and after that, your friend or foe, depending
on his bringing up.

—HASDAI IBN CRESCAS[1]

Becoming a father, much like becoming a man, is itself a prodigious task. It is often too all too easily signified by a narrow, observable event. So, we are led to believe that a man "becomes" a father when his female partner has given birth to the jointly conceived baby. Simple enough, or so it seems. In fact, however, becoming a father is a lengthy, often subtle, and highly complex process of development.

Becoming a father actually begins long before conception and birth. The roots of a woman's motherhood can be traced back to a little girl's wishes to become like her mommy and experience a maternal yearning to create through nurturance. Similarly, the foundations for a father's attachment and relationship to his infant can be observed in the little boy's nascent paternal identity, deriving from the instincts, wishes, and behaviors linked to both his parents.

But there is a psychobiology to fatherhood as well, a paternal instinct as it were, much as there is in motherhood. The term "genuine fatherliness" has been used to convey the instinctual roots of the male's capacity to develop fatherly ties and function as a provider.[2] These instinctual roots of fathering are manifest in his "engrossment" in his newborn: an altered state of consciousness that includes a sense of absorption, preoccupation, and interest in the infant that enables the father to feel enlarged.[3] A father is capable of achieving a "biorhythmic synchrony" with his infant, a kind of empathic nurturing similar to that displayed by mothers. In this, he appears to literally "take in" his baby in a bodily sense.[4] We often see similar responses in the little boy's nurturing and caretaking attitudes and behaviors toward his first puppy, turtle, or even goldfish. These early expressions of a boy's burgeoning fatherliness are strengthened considerably when his own father becomes actively engaged in nurturing him.

Unfortunately, more often than not, people tend to conceptualize pregnancy as being exclusively about the mother and her singular experience carrying a child. They correctly believe that the way in which she prepares herself, both psychologically and physically, has a profound influence on the baby. Yet at the same time, they mistakenly assume that a man's preparation will have little or no influence on the baby. Most fail to recognize that a man's relationship with his child *also* begins well before birth, and that a father also exerts a profound influence on both the pregnancy and how the child will ultimately turn out. Moreover, pregnancy affects the father in many unforeseen ways, so that he too has just as significant an experience during these nine months as his wife does.

Keith, a former patient of mine, discovered this quite early. He was seven when his baby sister was born and recalled that his own father, a professional musician, was "never around." Nonetheless, when his wife May told him that she was pregnant, Keith was ecstatic. They had always talked about having a family, but now that it was really about to happen, he could hardly contain himself; he told everyone he knew, even though May had asked him to keep it quiet for the first trimester, while thoughts of what life would be like with a new son or daughter preoccupied him constantly.

Keith anticipated that a new baby would foster changes in their lives even before the birth; but modeling himself on his own father, he did not imagine in the least that May's pregnancy would significantly interfere with his daily routines. He assumed that he'd still go to work without taking into account what might be needed at home, eat the dinners his wife prepared, visit his friends some weekday evenings until late, and of course, play softball on Saturday mornings. When May's fatigue and wildly fluctuating mood swings reached a peak, however, Keith began to fear what his life would be like once the baby actually arrived. He began to sense that he would have many new responsibilities for others besides himself, and worried about how his life would be further altered—would he have to give up his softball games and even more drastic, have to learn to cook?

As Keith and I discussed his anxieties, we both noticed how his instinctive sense of paternal nurturance took effect. He promptly realized how important it was for him to help May out during this time—that this was a way of setting the stage for the appearance of his child; he saw how much she needed him, and how she would need his help even more once the baby arrived. As a result, he volunteered to stay home on Saturday mornings, sitting on the couch with her as they read the newspaper and planned the evening's activity. He even taught himself how to cook simple meals and helped out more around the house.

With me, he shared how conflicted he felt about making personal sacrifices that he knew were necessary to help May during her pregnancy and beyond. He feared that he would no longer "be the man" that he was. At the same time, the changes May's pregnancy ushered in ultimately made him a far better husband and prepared him to be a caring and attentive father. Following his son's birth, he noted with irony that though he had no longer feared being who he used to be, he now proudly proclaimed himself a new man who had become a real father.

So in short, by altering his priorities and becoming an attentive caregiver to his wife, Keith realized that, through her, he could also take care of their child. Conversely, at the same time, the pregnancy was changing *him*. By becoming directly involved in the pregnancy through acting generously toward his wife, challenging assumptions derived from observing his father, and relinquishing some of his own needs in the interest of mother and child, Keith was able to expand his conceptions of manliness, parenthood, and what it means to be a more complete human being. Keith was indisputably becoming a father.

EMOTIONAL MANAGEMENT AND ACTING AS DELEGATE

Men become better husbands during this time in that they learn to work alongside their wives in a new way, as Keith did by assuming more household responsibilities. One way that a man accomplishes this is by becoming a "delegate" and taking on—or taking over—tasks and activities that had previously been within his wife's domain, and essentially becoming the "spokesperson" for the family. Accordingly, the woman, released from many of her outside world responsibilities, can withdraw and tend to the world inside her own body that requires her focus and care. Furthermore, to many men, becoming a delegate is a way for them to feel as though they are, in a sense, balancing the scale by contributing in a direct and immediate way to a situation in which their wives seem to be bearing the brunt. By being helpful, they are relieving the burden on their wives, which in the long term will be beneficial to all parties involved. In this way, a husband shields his pregnant wife (and fetus) from the impingement of the world, helping her to keep its demands at bay.

For example, one night Art, a father-to-be in a group I led, and his wife Joann, who was six months pregnant, were walking out of a movie theater when they spotted a woman Joann casually knew. This woman made a beeline for Joann. "I haven't seen you for a while and now I know why! You have quite a tummy there!" And with that, the woman placed her hand on Joann's belly, rubbing it. Joann was a private person and hated being touched; in fact, her distaste for casual physical contact and violation of her physical space had only deepened with her pregnancy. Art knew that Joann had a hard time speaking up when it came to issues like this, and given her internal focus during pregnancy, was especially reticent to assert herself at this time. Though Joann forced herself to smile at the woman, Art knew that his wife was cringing inside. He felt a strong need to protect both her and their baby, and thus, gently turned her body so the woman's hand would fall away from her stomach.

"Thanks for your good wishes," he said to the woman, "but

we've got to be getting home. Nice to see you . . ." And with that, he put his arm on his wife's shoulder and they began to walk away. In this simple but assertive way, Art served as delegate, protecting Joann from the woman's invasiveness by recognizing and communicating her needs and wishes when she couldn't. Art's appreciation of his wife's internal experience allowed him to be her advocate when she felt helpless or overwhelmed. His new role then, when necessary, was to act as his wife's voice, saying or doing what she might if she were up to it.

A less obvious way that a man grows as a result of his wife's pregnancy is by learning to essentially become her "emotional manager"; that is, he helps to hold or carry, contain, and modulate his wife's anxieties and emotions so that she is able to remain appropriately centered on and devoted to her growing fetus.

Sheila, for example, was eight months pregnant when she read an article in the science section of the newspaper about the controversy over acceptable limits of mercury in tuna fish, and whether or not this may be harmful to a fetus. She spent the day on the Internet trying to learn as much as she could about the issue, and by the time her husband David arrived home from work, she was terrified. She began to talk in a hurried frenzy about the tuna sandwich she had been having every week at work, and whether she had already damaged their child.

Having read the same article on his way to work, David was not without his own fears. At night, stirred into wakefulness by Sheila's restlessness, he was visited by many other anxieties, all related to whether or not their child would be born normal and healthy. Yet at this moment, with Sheila so anxious, he managed to keep his own fears to himself. In a calm tone, he reassured his wife that the article was talking about amounts of mercury way beyond the contents of a weekly tuna fish sandwich. He reiterated what all the doctors had told them—that because of their age and relative health, the odds of their having a healthy baby were quite good.

David realized that Sheila needed him to "hold" and keep in check her anxieties as well as his own, rather than stimulate them by allowing her to be overwhelmed by media-fueled worries. When David was able to successfully contain both of their anxieties, each of them felt relieved and better able to put their fears aside as much as they could.

By fulfilling these roles, men help to forge a special alliance with their wives during pregnancy, a relationship in which both are joined by strong empathic bonds to experience new levels of intense closeness, as they become increasingly engaged in the same task. By the time the baby is born, a man may not have to play the role of the delegate and emotional manager in quite the same way since most of the excessive physical demands of pregnancy on his wife will have lessened; however, he has learned from this role to be a more supportive and active husband. The close alliance grounded in emotional understanding fortifies the relationship between husband and wife, strengthening the foundation that is so necessary to give a baby a good beginning in the world. It forms the basis for what I call the "parenting alliance": a union formed out of their shared goals and particular similarities and differences that will continue throughout the child's development.

A FATHER'S CREATIVITY

A common tendency of expectant fathers is to focus solely on the fact that they are nothing but observers of the "main event," bystanders fated to witness the pregnancy secondhand. Although many men are proud of their ability to impregnate, which is the ultimate act of male creation, their unabashed pride can become supplanted by the sobering reality that the life they helped create grows in another's body. This can complicate men's feelings, driving them to experience jealousy, envy, and a sense of exclusion. Not only that, but because of pure biology, women innately come to know their children sooner and more intimately than men ever can.

Therefore, despite the joy, excitement, and vicarious pleasure the man might be feeling at this time, only the woman experiences the pregnancy in a bodily way. Because of this biological fact, it is often culturally expected that he experience the events of a pregnancy secondhand—that is, he remain relatively unaffected by it. He's always destined, at some level, to remain on the outside. In his book *When Men Are Pregnant,* the psychologist Jerrold Shapiro suggests that men are put in a "double bind," wherein they are encouraged to participate fully in their wives' pregnancies while at the same time, in virtual contradiction, they are also thought of as outsiders who are required to keep their feelings to themselves.[5] Yet how many men have you heard complain about this? Probably very few, if any. That is because our society does not encourage men to question their outsider status during pregnancy; actually, they experience considerable cultural pressure to deny it completely. Men are often not encouraged to help their wives in more than an ancillary way, nor are they encouraged to help *themselves* to understand their own, more subtle internal changes.

Accordingly, at this time, it is absolutely essential for the father as well as for his wife and unborn child that he seek out ways to feel what he knows intellectually to be true, namely, that the fact that the baby is maturing in another person's body does not make him any less of an important player in its creation, growth, and development. In order to neutralize his feelings of exclusion, envy, and loss in previously having been his wife's most significant *bodily* other, a father needs to successfully redirect these potentially destructive emotions into more socially valuable ones. Most men can accomplish this by finding their own, uniquely male mode of creating for themselves the experience that their partner is undergoing, even though it will be in a very different way.

I argue that, when husbands are able to find constructive, positive, and healthy ways to exercise their creativity—when they are able to see before their eyes the products they have invented with their own minds or hands—they are then more capable of putting aside feelings of exclusion, helplessness, worthlessness, and intense jealousy that will only serve as destructive forces in the family dynamic. Furthermore, I propose that only when fathers discover ways to satisfy their own needs for creativity can they genuinely share with their wives, in a non-conflicted way, the feelings of awe accompanying the end of pregnancy and the actual delivery.[6]

In my individual practice and in groups that I have led for fathers-to-be, I have encountered men who found constructive ways to reconcile these negative, troublesome sentiments. Sam, for example, worked in a bank, but had a woodworking shop set up in his basement, a hobby he had learned from his own father. During his wife's pregnancy, he waited until she retired to bed with a book before retreating to the basement, where he designed and built a cradle for their baby. Frank, a computer programmer, spent his free time creating a program he hoped to eventually teach his child. Juan, who was a sculptor, created a magnificent wooden statue to place in the nursery. By engaging in such varied types of activities, these men were essentially expressing the deepest internal urge to give birth to something inside them. Through these acts of creation, fathers find an adaptive, sublimated way to give life to the tiny evolving being growing inside the wives they love.

More than a few men, however, are unable to bear the responsibility and worry during this time and therefore struggle intensely with their anxieties and fears. For example, Stuart told the group that he was unable to sleep at night, becoming physically ill, haunted by worries that the fetus would come to harm. He became increasingly irritable and unsupportive of his wife. As the men in the group shared their reactions, Stuart realized that though his concerns were common, he had become dominated by them and needed an outlet for his feelings of helplessness, exclusion, and passivity. Stuart loved to write, especially poetry and songs, and with the encouragement of the others, he began to write stories and songs for his "baby boy." Shortly after investing himself in something that he could create, his worries and fears diminished.

Some men, particularly those with problematic attachment issues from their relationships with their own fathers and mothers that surface during this time, have more trouble finding outlets for their feelings. They instead find ways to leave the marriage, whether literally or figuratively. Perhaps the most familiar example of a father fleeing during pregnancy is the "workaholic" husband—the man who becomes addicted to work.

Rich was thirty-four when his wife Nancy, thirty-eight, became pregnant. When Rich heard the news, he felt very ambivalent—he wanted the opportunity to be a good father, and simultaneously felt terrified of the responsibilities. Nancy, on the other hand, welcomed the pregnancy with a huge sense of relief: for years, she'd described herself as "a natural mother," and fretted that her biological clock was running out. Rich, however, had misgivings about becoming a dad; in fact, he'd acceded to Nancy's wishes to have a child somewhat reluctantly. He didn't feel ready, emotionally or financially, to take this step. As the owner of his own small business, he threw himself into his work, putting in long hours and feeling increasingly depleted. Despite his considerable success, he felt even more driven by the idea of having to save up for the proverbial "rainy day"—especially now that a baby was on the way—and, in his estimation, he never seemed able to work hard enough.

Rich's behavior at this early stage of his wife's pregnancy had serious repercussions that manifested after the baby was born. Fortunately, he sought help from me for the deeper issues underlying his anxieties. Through our work together, he was able to overcome the obstacles that prevented him from participating actively in fathering his son. Indeed, for this to happen, the father (or the mother) needs to recognize his concerns about becoming a father as well as the detrimental symptoms of anxiety that bother him. But this is only the first step. Once a man acknowledges his misgivings, as both Stuart and Rich did, he needs to find methods to deal with them before he acts out in a destructive way.

In preparing for the birth of a child, confronted by new and demanding situations, men react in a variety of ways. Some have difficulty adapting to their new expectations and roles. More often than not, however, men are able to meet the challenge of impending fatherhood. In the process, these men discover that not only do they become more fulfilled as people, but that they are also ultimately ensuring their sons or daughters will have a healthy beginning. Those men who are able to recognize and learn how to constructively contain their anxieties about becoming fathers will most likely go on to enjoy a positive relationship with their children, and, as we'll see in the next chapter, will find themselves well prepared for actual fatherhood from the moment their child is born.

2

A FATHER IS BORN

*I cannot think of any need in childhood as
strong as the need for a father's protection.*

—SIGMUND FREUD[1]

For many fathers, witnessing the end of pregnancy and the actual delivery is an awesome, ineffable experience. Finally, after nine long months, the veil of mystery lifts: the baby is there to be held, touched, fed, and adored. Many find it hard to express the magnitude of their new emotion. Birth, that powerful, miraculous beginning, is often more than they ever dreamed. For some, it's their first experience of the transcendent—of something that goes beyond their ability to control. Some describe birth as sublime; others feel terrified. And though these feelings are often soon enough tempered by the reality of dirty diapers, colic, and sleepless nights, the sense of marvel lingers. During the earliest phases of a child's life, fathers become engrossed with their children whether they are boys or girls. My firstborn, Maya, was born after a difficult fourteen-hour labor during which I didn't leave my wife Linda's side. But as soon as the baby appeared and was eventually nestled in her mother's arms, I nearly burst with pride and exhilaration. Unable to contain my joy, I rushed out of the hospital and onto the street, greeting those I passed as if they were all beloved relatives. First I found a pay phone to call nearly everyone I knew—and some people I hardly knew at all—to describe the successful delivery and Maya's health and extraordinary beauty. I knew I sounded as if this was the first recorded human birth, but I couldn't stop myself. Then I found a store where I purchased more candy, flowers, and balloons than I could carry, knowing full well that Linda wasn't in the mood to eat anything, let alone pay attention to anything except her daughter. Even now, more than two decades later, no moment compares to the elation I felt on that morning when I met my daughter for the first time.

Seeing his own imprint on his infant son or daughter, a man projects himself onto his child and then elevates his boy or girl as an ideal being. That is, he regards his child as special in the same ways that he wants to be recognized as special himself. This may sound grandiose. But in fact, it's what the psychoanalyst Peter Wolson calls "adaptive grandiosity."[2] The term refers to those nourishing yet commonly extravagant feelings that allow the father to feel passionately connected to his young son or daughter. I regard this natural and healthy facet of parenting as a kind of "narcissism in the service of connection." It is something we see all the time when we observe loving fathers and mothers with their little ones—something I saw in myself after my own daughter's birth. Moreover, this phenomenon evidences that whatever the nature of a father's unique bond is with *his son*, it in no way precludes the significance of his intense and loving connection with *his daughter* (nor need it lead him to an overvaluation of his son and boys in general, along with a devaluation of his daughter and girls in general).

A father who can protect his wife and the mother-child bond while becoming engrossed with his child is simultaneously able to experience a loving union with the world and to acknowledge the fact of the world's otherness. This leads him to experience a deep sense of connection with life, and to appreciate his own unique place in the world.

The extent and quality with which fathers become involved with their infants affect the way these children develop. At the same time, these tiny, vulnerable beings exert a huge influence on their fathers. By accepting their caretaking and nurturing roles, many men discover opportunities to develop aspects of their personalities they may have previously ignored while incorporating traits they may have formerly eschewed.

THE "GOOD ENOUGH" FATHER

Fatherliness has instinctual roots; indeed, most every man has the capacity to develop fatherly ties that render his relationship to his child a mutual developmental experience. Despite its instinctual basis, however, the specific benefits of fatherhood don't come so automatically. Whether we attribute it to biology, culture, or a combination of both, many men, unlike women, need to learn to become responsible fathers and to guide their sons along the same pathway. As the French philosopher Jean-

Jacques Rousseau noted in a remark during the mid-1700s that still rings true today, the mother-child bond is fully *natural,* while the father-child bond must be *cultivated.*[3] Indeed, treating fathers as the "forgotten" parent may be an outcome of the cultural penchant for favoring a mother's "nature" over a father's more often hard-earned ability to nurture.

One of the ways men can cultivate this bond is by becoming actively engaged in the lives of their children. This involvement can't be restricted to external activities, like changing diapers or attending school plays. First and foremost, it must be extended to their children's *internal lives,* particularly their subjective, more emotional experience. To accomplish this, fathers simultaneously need to value and attend to their own internal lives as well, which includes their emotions, impulses, thoughts, wishes, beliefs, and memories and impressions. By attending to his own inner life, a father is provided with the understanding that will enable him to recognize his child's subjectivity.

Fathers who are willing to face themselves in these ways are on the route to being "good enough." According to the eminent British pediatrician and psychoanalyst D. W. Winnicott, who coined the term in reference to the mother, "good enough" does not refer to a parent who is only adequate or serviceable, one who does only what is "enough."[4] Rather, Winnicott is referring to a mother whose relationship with her child is close enough to promote psychological growth but not too close to smother the child. Similarly, a "good enough" father negotiates such a middle path with his children so as to guide and mentor them by helping them regulate their emotions, achieve mastery, and take on the challenges of the world at large. Specifically, he helps them experience life's more difficult moments—such as loss, frustration, and disappointment—in ways that promote and enhance rather than inhibit growth. He does this by recognizing a quality that psychologists call "otherness." That is, he has the ongoing capacity to see his children as individuals who exist in their own right without reference to him, and who have their own separate internal, subjective worlds. The "good enough" father is an ideal that is within reach; men can become "good enough" through their own choices and conscious effort. These fathers demand of themselves, and of their children, only what can be honestly given.

In becoming a good enough father, men do find themselves growing more empathic, vulnerable, and trusting—qualities that our culture often stereotypes as "feminine." In the past, men may have avoided or disavowed these qualities as seemingly at odds with what it meant to be a man or to be successful. By becoming fathers, however, men have the opportunity to confront and reintegrate such qualities into their personalities so that they can care for their children. As a result, they can experience themselves as more whole. They also feel freer to nurture and attune to the needs of others, and to skillfully use their paternal authority and masculine aggression in constructive ways.

There are various tasks a father must fulfill in order to be a good enough father, tasks that require a father to recognize what his son needs from him at specific junctures in his son's developmental journey. I will discuss and explore these provisions and phases in the son's and father's development throughout this book. All of these tasks are essential to ensuring the healthy development of a son or daughter. Indeed, the absence of sufficient good enough fathering is likely to produce specific consequences at each developmental junction, such as particular conflicts and deficits, often manifest in the painful affective state of yearning known as "father hunger."[5]

My framework for understanding the nature of good enough

fathering considers the roles a father assumes in response to his son's needs, beginning when the child is first conceived and moving forward in time until death. Each of these roles and phases will be explored in subsequent chapters. During pregnancy and the first months of life, as I maintained in chapter 1 and will elaborate in this chapter, a father functions as a *guardian*, or watchful, protective presence. In the first years of life, a father becomes "the second other," the parent who, in his role as *liaison*, is able to pull the baby out of the exclusive orbit with the mother into the larger world. As the son reaches the preschool years, a father acts as a *model* for and *sanctioner* of his son's nascent sense of masculinity. During the "oedipal years," when the son starts school, a father works as a *challenger,* helping his son learn to rein in and manage his impulses and strong emotions, while *guiding* him to compete in healthy ways. In the middle of childhood, a father becomes a *mentor* to his growing son, teaching him a sense of mastery over things while initiating him into the world of men. In adolescence, a father becomes a *hero*, embodying all the traits the boy aspires to. During later adolescence, a father becomes a *fallen hero*, as his teenage son needs to break away and renounce what his father stands for. As the young man reaches early adulthood, a father reprises his role as a *mentor* to adult manhood, easing this difficult transition. A man becoming middle-aged will turn to his father as an *aging equal* and very often a *wise elder* in traversing the tides of later adulthood. And finally, when the son enters late middle age, his elderly father becomes an *aging elder,* who often depends on his son as his son once did on his father, while the father helps to prepare his son to face his own end-of-life issues.

. . .

WATCHFUL PROTECTOR

The wish to be watched over and protected is among the most archaic and universal of desires. This fundamental longing to be tended to and provided for is experienced by an individual in both imaginary and actual relationships with others, from birth throughout the life span. These watchful others include mothers, grandparents, and older siblings, in addition to societal, political, and symbolic leaders. Despite the breadth of these roles, however, the preeminent representation of such a protector and provider is that of the father.

The task of serving as a "watchful protector" is part of the definition of "real manhood" across many cultures and traditions, and is perhaps the preeminent characteristic of fatherhood from which all other characteristics are derived.[6] The anthropologist David D. Gilmore, who has studied the concept of masculinity throughout the world, notes that the vast majority of cultures regard the male's role as having, in addition to impregnating his wife, two other essential purposes—to protect and provide:

> Men nurture their society by shedding their blood, their sweat, and their semen, by bringing home food for both child and mother, by producing children, and by dying if necessary in faraway places to provide a safe haven for their people.[7]

While this example might be read as a bit extreme from our cultural standpoint, the notion that men are expected to act as strong and assertive authority figures holds true even in our society where many women hold jobs and serve as primary wage earners. Even children living in non-traditional households, where the father is the primary caretaker and the mother is the main source of income, still grow up believing that men are the ones who singularly protect and provide. This should indicate just how strong and ubiquitous are our cultural representations of masculinity, how even in the twenty-first century we cannot rid our minds of the gender stereotypes that have been so strongly and unwaveringly enforced until only recently.

Accordingly, when a father is unable to live up to this cultural and symbolic father ideal, undue damage is done to his child's emotional and social development as well as to his own self-ideal and sense of self-worth. In contrast, through his providing and protecting functions, the "actual" father is largely able to fulfill the ideal of the more "symbolic" father.

From an evolutionary perspective, human fathers, like many animal fathers, have evolved to care for and feed their partners and children, to love and protect their partners and children, and to stay with and *not* abandon them. The notion of the good father, the sky father, the father who protects and guides, is not unique among humans, but exists even across the species, which speaks to the argument that there's an instinct for fathering. As the cultural analyst Jeffrey Masson writes:

> "This child is mine, I will take care of her," says the male emperor penguin, the male sea horse, the Scottish father, the Jamaican father, the father wolf, the male mouthbrooding teleost fish, the Indonesian father, the male tamarin, the father from Berkeley, California, the father from India, father beaver, father prairie dog, the male Darwin frog from Argentina, the Chilean father, and even

(back into our past) the ancient Egyptian father,
the Sumerian father, the Neanderthal father.[8]

Therefore, while a father's impact as watchful protector may
seem abstract and indirect, it could not be more real or crucial.
When fathers oversee their wives' and children's emotional and
physical well-being, mothers are freed up to concentrate directly
on the immediate needs of their baby. The more a mother feels
shielded from excessive worries and anxieties, as well as from
unnecessary distractions and extraneous concerns, the better
she is able to help her baby develop a strong sense of self.

The father helps his infant to develop a secure attachment to
the mother by providing a timely and nurturing holding environment for both mother and infant. This paternal holding, characterized by the supportive continuity that the father provides,
facilitates what the dependent infant needs from the mother-
child relationship, the mother's primary attunement.[9] Especially
before the infant can make use of him in other ways, the watchful father frees the mother to devote herself to the baby. In holding the mother-infant dyad near the end of pregnancy and for
several weeks after the baby's birth, the father is able to promote
the mother's "primary maternal preoccupation," which is necessary for her to minister optimally to her child's needs and
thereby become the basis for the infant's ego establishment.[10]

Also, this initial paternal presence of protective watchfulness,
when accompanied by subsequent "good enough" fatherly
involvement and provision, proceeds to evolve and develop
alongside other fatherly representations over the life cycle.
Thus, the involved father who is able to watch over, hold, and
protect the mother and her small child is likely in due course to
become the father who protects and encourages his young toddler's separation and individuation from the mother, as I will dis-

cuss in later chapters. Similarly, years later, he must again hold,
bear, and support with interested restraint his adolescent's identity experimentation and subsequent distancing from family
dependencies. For the time being, he also enables the emotional
relationship between the mother and her new baby to begin and,
subsequently, to develop naturally. The progressive, developmental accomplishments that depend upon this fatherly contribution increase the chances that, even in a grown child's mid-
to late adulthood, a healthy, internal sense of being watched
over will remain vibrantly alive.

However, children of fathers who are unable to provide sufficient protective agency during the earliest phases of their lives
are less likely to receive important fatherly provisions at the later
stages, even though there are subsequent opportunities for
parental contributions. The provision of sufficient paternal protective agency early in children's lives is quite pressing, and its
absence has wide-ranging social and psychological implications.
There is evidence, for example, that children of fathers who are
decidedly less involved in these initial phases of fathering are
more likely during later childhood and adult development to
incur incestuous sexual abuse, paternal abandonment, and the
detrimental effects of uninvolved or ineffective fathering, including "father hunger."[11]

This is illustrated in the case of Sarah, a middle-aged woman
in the latter stages of a lengthy psychoanalysis. During our work
together, she had made considerable progress in coming to terms
with her severely traumatic early childhood—characterized by
her father's inability to provide sufficient protection from an abusive relative—and ultimately with her accompanying psychic
demons. At one point in her treatment, she arrived for her session reporting that she felt extremely angry with her husband
"without having any idea why." She noted the "irrationality" of

her anger before lamenting "how hard life is and how much evil there is in the world."

As the session proceeded, Sarah described an upsetting incident that had occurred earlier that week. She had purchased a black Raiders football team jacket for her first-grade son and presented it to him. He was quite pleased and Sarah felt good about making the purchase. Later that afternoon, her husband returned and informed them that the jacket and team insignia were worn by a Los Angeles gang and that, consequently, it would be dangerous for their son to wear it. She proclaimed indignantly, "Can you imagine how fucked up the world is that little children could be shot just for wearing certain colors?" She cried in remarking how her small son's "innocence and trust couldn't be protected."

As Sarah's associations continued, it soon became apparent that she blamed her husband for somehow not seeing to it that the world was safe enough for their son to wear the logo of his favorite football team. She berated her husband for not being stronger and earning more money. "Why can't he have everything under control and know exactly what he's doing," she asked, "so we could live wherever we want, have our kids in private schools, and not have to worry at all about bad things happening to us?" She then tearfully acknowledged that he was a good, loving father nonetheless.

Within a short time, Sarah could see how enraged she was toward her husband, as well as toward me, for not being "someone who could make [her] feel completely safe, secure, and protected." As we fleshed out her wishes together, she began to experience and understand more deeply how she had always longed for a father who could provide such watchful protection. She could recognize how these childhood yearnings were transferred to both her husband and her analyst, each of whom became the object of her bitter disappointment, fear, and rage.

This vindictive yet unconscious rage toward men, to whom she transferred her frustrated childhood longings for her father's protectiveness, left her feeling completely alone and unsafe in a modern-day reenactment of her early inner life.

RECONCILING MANLINESS WITH TAKING A "BACKSEAT" ROLE

Some fathers, like Sarah's, are too removed to exert a significant influence on their children's lives. Other fathers struggle with their need to remain in the background more than they would like. These men need to learn how to use their manliness in a positive and productive manner, one that will ultimately help them to be better fathers. When a man finds himself in situations in which mother and child are an autonomous unit, self-sufficient and content, he is essentially forced into a "backseat" role, one that he may erroneously perceive as passive. He often finds his job of protecting and supporting the mother-child bond to conflict with his desire to indulge his self-centered need to be "the man"—the one at the wheel, the one in dominating control.

This conflict can activate his impulse to deny the reality of his wife and child's needs in order to maintain his own more narcissistically based form of masculinity that requires active control and vanquishing. In such a case, this man might become depressed or frequently act out by having affairs, abandoning his family, losing himself to work, or generally becoming unavailable as a watchful protector in the father's version of postpartum depression. The tragic quality of such failed fathering is compounded by the male's sense of shame and guilt surrounding his arrested sense of manhood.

In the ideal situation, however, the father is able to recognize that in his role as a watchful protector, holding his wife and child from the outside, he *is*, in fact, directly contributing not only to a positive family dynamic but also to the healthy development of his child. He can even begin to see that fatherhood offers him the chance to accept and integrate disparate sides of himself into a more inclusive, flexible, and yet cohesive sense of manliness, rather than disavow or repress the parts that do not seem to fit. A man enters into his infant's world and learns what it means to be a father by subduing his own more egoistic needs—sublimating his masculine inclinations for self-centeredness and acquisition—in order to see and meet the needs of his child. Accordingly, he reaches a new level of self-understanding that he would not have arrived at had he not become a father.

For some men, perhaps, this is the first time that their inner lives come into focus more clearly than their outer lives. Relationships and intimacy become as important as performance and achievement. However, this understanding may not come so easily. Men are trained to be "doers," to tackle issues and solve problems. They like to feel useful, active, and productive. Yet, as new fathers, they often find themselves in situations in which mother and baby are a unit unto themselves. With no pressing problems to solve, dads are often asked to act in ways that they perceive as relatively passive: to be a watchful presence, to protect and support the mother-child bond. Instead of thinking of themselves as standing alone, they are asked to fit themselves into the new three-way relationship they are sheltering.

But this period of relative inactivity can be seen as an opportunity for growth and gain. New fathers have the opportunity to realize that masculinity is not so much about remaining strong and solitary, but rather more about connecting with others while allowing them to exist separately and thrive. They learn that

their seemingly competing needs and characteristics—to be
dominant and aggressive, to achieve and be creative, and to be
loving and nurturing—don't cancel one another out, but can
comfortably coexist and in fact complement one another.
I once led a fathers' group with a former star athlete. He'd been
an engine of competition on the football field; to him, winning the
game was the only thing that mattered. Yet here's how he described
to his fathers' group the experience of being a new father:

> I watched them [his wife and child] playing with
> each other and I knew that I would destroy
> something they were sharing if I made my pres-
> ence known. It was difficult though to just
> watch; I wanted to get in there and do something
> . . . maybe toss my daughter up in the air or
> tickle her. I resisted the temptation though and I
> am glad. That evening, I noticed that I felt "older
> and heavier," not so "light and spry." But you
> know, I felt more like a man that night than I
> ever have, even when I kicked butt on the foot-
> ball field.

Taking more of a background position, however, does not pre-
clude a father from experiencing a new form of joyfulness. This
instinctual response is evident in a letter sent to me by Ricky, a
new father and former patient, describing his initial experience
of bonding with his newborn son Benji:

> I never could have imagined I would feel this
> jazzed about the little person sleeping swaddled
> next to me right now. I love looking at him,
> mashing my face against his, giving him kisses.

> No matter how cluttered my life feels, Benji is
> like the door to some higher dimension where
> the cares of this world are laughably irrelevant. I
> look at him—I never want to stop looking at
> him—and my stomach flutters.

Ricky's experience is not an uncommon example of a father's extravagant feelings of passionate connection that help draw him closer to his newborn child. The father's elation keeps him on course to provide the watchful protectiveness and emotional attunement that will facilitate his child's development.

In addition to being a watchful protector, the father can take on another "outside" role and become an "emotional manager" by very quickly becoming attuned to his baby's emotional needs. In fact, as I noted in the first chapter, the developmental psychoanalyst Teresa Benedek concluded that fatherhood has psychobiological roots; she speculated about an instinctual trait called "genuine fatherliness," which is released through a father's earliest contact with his young child, enabling him to respond with immediate empathy.[12] If true, this speaks even more profoundly to the importance of a father acting as the force to maintain emotional balance and harmony.

The father also serves as an indirect emotional manager for his baby by respecting his wife's preeminent emotional need: to free her from distraction so she can become preoccupied with the baby. This way, she develops an astonishing capacity to identify with her baby and thereby become exquisitely sensitive to the baby's basic needs. This exclusive dedication and devotion is crucial to the early stages of life and plays a pivotal role in the baby's development.

At the same time, the mother's devotion or preoccupation can best develop because her husband is actively safeguarding it. If each parent succeeds at this task, then the baby will most likely benefit from what the British developmental psychiatrist John Bowlby called "a secure base" from which all future development unfolds.[13] According to Bowlby, this secure base is a kind of crucible from which an emotionally stable person develops and functions throughout life. Children who grow up in such a safe haven know, as they venture into the larger world, that they can always return home if they need to and feel welcomed. Expressly because the father took a step back and allowed his wife to share a special bond with their child (thanks in part to the new level of selflessness he developed during his wife's pregnancy and which he continues to expand upon), he is "setting the stage," so to speak, for their child's healthy development.

Nonetheless, this may not be enough, since the child's healthy development also depends on the nature of the parents' relationship. Many mothers experience dramatic shifts in their own libidinal lives when so completely attuned to their babies. As a result, a father is frequently called upon to invite his wife to return to their conjugal relationship so that she learns to divide more of her focus between the maternal and spousal parts of herself. In so doing, a father is protecting both his wife's bond with their baby and the adult sexuality and intimacy in the marriage. Through his firm yet sensitive efforts to restore their suspended sexuality, he uses his manliness to strengthen his connection with his wife. By being both a *caring father* and an *exciting lover* to his wife, a vital anchor is provided for both his child and partner.[14] This imparts an integral link that joins both parents together and sets a young son on track toward establishing a secure sense of himself with his mother, with his father, and with his mother and father *together*.[15]

$\bullet \quad \bullet \quad \bullet$

FATHERS AND SONS

Until this point, I have been speaking about the influence felt by
fathers in relation to their children, be they sons or daughters.
Since this book is, in fact, about fathers in relation to their
sons—and I will focus more exclusively on this particular bond
as the book progresses—I should take a moment here to introduce briefly the ways in which, as time passes and babies grow,
the sex of the child does begin to make a difference in terms of
the relationship that develops with the father. Watching and
interacting with his young son, a father senses a deep connection
through a biological sameness, namely, their maleness.

Because a father naturally identifies more with a boy than
with a girl, he is able to better appreciate his son's nascent needs
for separateness and autonomy as a "male" person. That is, as a
man, the father has an intuitive understanding of his son's need
to separate from his primary relationship with his mother and
consequently begin to explore the larger world; he knows that
this very separation from the mother is fundamental to the boy's
sense of his "masculine" self. It's upon this understanding that
the child, as he grows, will be able to conceptualize himself as
apart from his parents. In other words, a son's autonomy develops from his father's belief in and empathetic support for this
autonomy. This phenomenon demonstrates the depth of the
father-son bond; even in these early stages, their connection is
real and profound, and essential to making sure the son grows up
feeling comfortable with himself, especially as a *male* person, as
well as with whatever differences he might possibly set up
between himself and his parents.

Oftentimes, however, it is difficult for fathers in these early stages of parenthood to find a way to connect to their young sons, due to certain internal conflicts they must reconcile. This was certainly true for Rich, the "workaholic" father discussed in the last chapter who was so ambivalent about having a child. Following his son Daniel's birth, Rich became noticeably agitated and depressed, and began arranging for increased traveling and other activities that kept him busy outside the home. As his ambivalence about his feelings of becoming a father had been largely repressed, despite having fathered the son that he "had always wanted," Rich not surprisingly felt terrible about himself "as a man." As he explained, things had become more and more unpleasant for him at home because his wife, Nancy, when not exhausted, "always seemed busy" with their infant. Rich complained vehemently about Nancy's "devotion" to Daniel and angrily deplored her "lack of interest either in me or in sex."

Rich was well into his second year of analysis with me when his son was about eight months old. Rich's wife had become increasingly enraged over his absences from the family and continued unavailability; Rich, in turn, began to struggle with how ashamed and cowardly he felt about his withdrawal from the life of his wife and child. He realized that he was repeating his own father's pattern, which he recalled as "leaving me all alone in the hands of my crazy mother, who poked me incessantly. Thank God Nancy's not crazy," he continued, "but still I can't stand watching her give so much love to Daniel while I feel so unloved and devalued."

In exploring Rich's shameful withdrawal, he realized that he had made Nancy into an ideal version of his own mother while abandoning her as both a mate and a lover. We discovered together that he had recreated the sense of being a little boy left alone without a father's watchful protectiveness toward his son and his marriage. Lacking an internal, "watchful" parental presence throughout his growth and development, Rich could not safely be alone without the idealized mother he made Nancy into and desperately clung to. Rich could only experience himself as "whole" when he was able to relive the illusion of completely satisfying his own mother, and consequently, reexperience himself as having recovered the "lost paradise" of being inside her.

We analyzed how Rich's sense of masculinity and accompanying self-esteem were linked to his fantasy of having his wife all to himself and, in turn, experiencing her as the source of his longed-for return to an ideal state of happiness. Rich gradually became more able to recognize, disclose, and bear his deep sense of shame and abandonment in his analysis as he understood that his experiences were connected to "phallic" ideals born out of childhood grandiosity. As a result, Rich's need to withdraw from Daniel and Nancy could lessen and he began to identify with Daniel as a self-extension in need of protective, involved fathering.

Rich recognized both how much his son needed a father who could "be the umbrella for Danny and his mother," and that Nancy needed a husband who joined her emotionally and welcomed her sexually in their conjugal bed. He mused as to how Daniel would need him in the years ahead, while genuinely appreciating Nancy's capacity to give so much love to their son. And eventually, he was able to reclaim his wife as partner and become a father to Daniel.

Watching and interacting with his son, a father senses deep connection—a biological sameness, their maleness—qualities that he doesn't share with his daughter. It's not only to a father's advantage to recognize his son's essential separateness; this recognition helps the son as well by facilitating his autonomy.

Even so, accepting the otherness of one's son isn't always easy.

Harold, for example, a muscular thirty-five-year-old former professional athlete, had assumed primary care of one-year-old Darius when his wife, Felicia, went back to work as an anesthesiologist. A proud man, Harold struggled considerably with the reversal of roles, particularly since he was not earning much money as a freelance sports trainer while Felicia was earning both considerable income and respect in her field. To make matters worse, eighteen-month-old Darius was not talking and did not respond to simple directions. Harold's attempts to "discipline" him with rules and firmness only made Darius more agitated. No matter what he did, Harold could not seem to connect to or comfort his son.

By the time Darius was two, his parents were quite concerned about his disinterest in other children and his inability to speak. Sensing a more serious problem, the family pediatrician referred the child to a specialist, who diagnosed Darius with autistic spectrum disorder.

Harold was devastated by the news and became very depressed. He couldn't understand how his boy wasn't capable of learning to talk, listen, or respond more normally to "clear-cut rules." His own sense of manhood, already compromised by his wife's success in the world along with his difficulties adjusting to the life of being an ex-professional athlete, made it very hard for Harold to be around Darius.

But he had no choice. Darius—and Felicia—needed him more than ever. In particular, they needed Harold to relinquish some of his cherished beliefs of manhood in order to deal with his son's needs. Luckily, Harold was a guy who prided himself on "never quitting on anyone or anything." He vowed to stand by his son— and he did. By attending every speech therapy session, he learned how to communicate with Darius, a child who didn't rely on the usual interpersonal cues Harold took for granted. He learned to help his son engage in games like peek-a-boo and pat-a-cake that would help Darius ultimately learn to use language. Despite his limitations, Darius responded very well to his father's increasingly gentle and patient care. Within a few months, the boy had made progress that even the experts had not expected.

But most remarkable of all, according to Darius's speech and language therapist, was Harold's transformation. "I couldn't relate to him when we first met," the therapist said. "He was so controlled and macho, and he didn't listen. He acted like only he knew exactly what Darius needed. But over the year of our work, Harold really changed. It was as if he became a trainer of himself. I saw a sensitivity and softness emerge in him that helped Darius begin to flourish. Now, I'd consider Harold to be one of the best fathers that I've ever encountered."

As Harold described it, he realized that there were many ways of being a man, and many ways of winning. "You can't always be the strongest, toughest, or most controlled," he explained. "Sometimes you have to find another way to get what you want." As Darius became much more responsive, so did his dad. Each taught the other. Each had much to learn.

The benefits of being an engaged father—to both father and son—are irrefutable. Fathers who remain actively involved with their sons can take comfort in knowing that they are making perhaps the most important investment in their own and their child's future they possibly can. For it is very likely that their boys will grow up to be adults for whom the internal sense of being watched over, protected, and provided for, even as they become parents and grandparents themselves, will remain vibrantly alive.

Those men who are able to watch over, hold, and protect

their wives and sons will find that they are called on to persist in these roles in the years ahead. At every developmental stage, new challenges will emerge, and men wishing to remain engaged with their sons will need to adapt their stance of watchful protectiveness to keep in step with their child's maturational needs and the constantly changing nature of their relationship. In the next few years, for example, fathers become an even more pivotal presence, and the degree to which they are willing to be engaged with their sons becomes crucial. As I'll discuss in the next chapter, the father's emerging role as the "second other"—that is, a different, loving presence who isn't the mother—is essential for development. It's through the father as a "second other" that the small boy begins to experience his emerging sense of uniqueness and differentiation from his mother, a crucial developmental milestone.

3

FATHERS INTRODUCING
TODDLERS TO THE WORLD

For in the baby lies the future of the world.
Mother must hold the baby close so that the
baby knows it is his world. Father must
take him to the highest hill so that he can
see what his world is like.

—MAYAN INDIAN PROVERB[1]

As their young children begin to emerge from early infancy, fathers come forward as the "second other" who will initially impact their lives by introducing them to the world.[2] A father's involvement as a loving and engaged presence that is different than the mother enables his child to begin to experience his own emerging sense of separateness from his mother in a less distressing fashion. The child is also learning that others, like his father, can be there to provide for him when his mother is unavailable.

Recognizing and affirming his child's "otherness" is a task for which fathers are particularly well suited—surprisingly, in some ways better suited than women. A father helps create this new life, yet his child is not "of" him in the same way that the child is "of" the mother. From the very beginning, holding his child in his arms, the engaged father says to himself, "This child is me, but also is not me." Because of this initial bodily differentiation, fathers are positioned to more fully recognize and celebrate their children as separate individuals.

Fathers have a unique and special way of encouraging their young children to leave the nest. For example, fathers tend to play with their infants and small children in more stimulating, vigorous, novel, and unpredictable ways than mothers do since they relate to their babies in a different fashion. According to Dan Siegel, a child psychiatrist who studies brain development, a baby's mind develops as much from exploring interpersonal processes as it does from other types of physical stimulation.[3] Siegel's research suggests that mothers' interpersonal energy is centripetal, drawing the baby inward, while fathers' energy is centrifugal, away from the center, more toward the outer world. Fathers tend to be more challenging, whereas mothers do more soothing—in short, by arousing and shifting the child's state to fit his own, a father attunes to his child in a "disruptive" fashion in contrast to a mother's "homeostatic attunement."[4]

Small children may not notice their fathers and the challenge they represent until they have attained a certain maturity. When they reach this point and fathers are engaged, as in the following example, the small boy can virtually smell the scent of adventure on his father's clothing as the boy's sense of exploration is fostered.

I recall observing a young married couple walking their two-year-old son Ian to a neighborhood park. At the park, I saw that Eve, the mother, packed a blanket and Ian's favorite books for them to read while the father, Tom, started jogging. Ian seemed content sitting with his mom as she read to him.

But suddenly, as soon as Ian saw his father returning from his run, he began to squirm. By the time Tom reached the blanket, Ian could hardly contain himself. "Daddy, play!" he said. Together, father and son began running to the swings. "Higher!" Ian squealed as Tom began pushing him. "Higher!" Ian threw back his head in sheer delight.

Eve watched father and son from the blanket. I imagined that she was recalling how sweetly and calmly Ian had been sitting with her just a few moments ago. Suddenly, as she observed Tom and Ian heading for the monkey bars, she abruptly came to her feet, shouting, "He's not ready for that." Eve started running toward the play equipment, anxious and afraid. "He'll be fine, don't worry," Tom said. Eve hesitated, then smiled, and walked over to a nearby bench so she could relax and still have a good view of her husband and son enjoying their time together.

A small boy's energized, newfound relationship with his father, though it may appear sudden, reflects a universal dynamic that can be traced back to mythic tales from cultures across the globe. According to one legend from India, for example, a mother joyfully sits holding her baby and says, "I will comfort you." The father then takes the baby to the mountaintop and eagerly proclaims, "This is the world; I will introduce you!" In ancient Greece, Zeus, king of the gods, is depicted as the "sky father," who rules the heavens from high on Mount Olympus, thunderbolt in hand, guardian of law and order on earth, upholder of fatherly and kingly authority.

Of course, in today's rapidly changing social climate, an

increasing number of mothers more actively introduce their baby to the world while fathers assume the primary nurturer role. The qualities of being motherly and caretaking, as well as achievement-oriented and outer-directed, naturally transcend gender. However, in this book, I will discuss mothers and fathers in a more culturally based, conventional, even archetypal mode: the mother (or her surrogate) as the link to the inner, emotional world, while the father is the tie to the outer, physical world.

FATHERS INTRODUCE THEIR SONS
TO THE LARGER WORLD

The father's earliest role in his child's life is to aid in his or her struggle to differentiate from the mother. To begin to understand this phenomenon, think of a budding toddler as looking at the world as if it were a photograph in the process of being developed. Until now, only one object can be discerned with any clarity: the mother. And while the mother's identity is so closely merged with that of the baby, there's almost no telling where one begins and the other ends. The father is only a shadowy presence off to the side. By the child's second year, however, the blur comes into sharper focus, and the toddler begins to understand that there is someone else in the equation (or picture, to finish off the metaphor). At this moment, the father steps out of the shadows and takes his place in his child's life, assuming the important role of the "second other."

The baby welcomes this introduction to a "new" type of parent. Between the ages of eighteen months to three years of age, a child's physical, emotional, and social awareness develop at almost breakneck speed. This physiological and psychological growth has enormous and very visible repercussions. Babies who have previously been content to sit with their mothers begin to get squirmy, like restless unborn chicks kicking at the confines of their shells. The formerly comforting world of the nursery begins to feel cloying. The exclusive relationship with the mother becomes a bit claustrophobic. Babies are ready for more stimulation that will alter the way they think, feel, perceive, and move.

In some cases, the father assumes the task of coaxing, luring, and sometimes even pushing his child out of the mother's nurturing orbit. Men are often particularly well suited for this task precisely because they do not experience the intense psychobiological intermingling that the mother does with her baby both during gestation and post-birth lactation and feeding.

It doesn't matter how much babies are maturing physiologically or how powerfully the outside world tantalizes them; many are still reluctant to leave the comforting and secure world of the nursery. However, without a father or surrogate's steadfast encouragement, some children may ultimately never entirely leave their mothers' arms. The child with an involved father can more easily realize that staying in the nursery is neither the sole nor most desirable option.

At a certain point, all babies begin to notice their fathers, thereby perceiving the world with an entirely new lens. This is especially significant for boys because not only are they separating *emotionally* from their mothers, but they are simultaneously noticing that they are *physically* different from them. Boys wish that they were the same as both their mothers and fathers, but as they become increasingly aware of genital and gender differences, they see that their bodies resemble their fathers', not their mothers'. Realizing that they are *not* like their mothers in a variety of ways can be terrifying: boys cannot console themselves as girls can by reassuring themselves that their bodily similarities with their mothers provide a sense of sameness despite the growing difference. Many boys have extreme difficulty reconciling this dilemma and require the active presence of a father (or his surrogate) to cushion the blow.

By becoming actively and intimately engaged with his son, securely affirming the reality of gender differences, the father offers his boy a mirror; peering into it, his son sees himself. Encouraged to identify with his father, the boy begins to explore his own nascent masculinity. Reassured, he's ready to recognize the changes that he is experiencing, and through the connection with his dad, the young boy begins incorporating these changes into his life.

Little boys are enamored with their fathers—a "second other"—and seek to emulate them in any way they can. For example, sometime during the second or third year when children give up diapers and learn to use the toilet, sons rely on their fathers to model bathroom behavior. You can see this whenever a little boy stands at the toilet with his dad, trying to make bubbles with his urine as Dad does, or standing next to his dad while he shaves.

Moreover, fathers who are engaged with their sons can help them to better handle the uncertainty as well as the painful, conflicted feelings that arise during this time of transition in separating from their mothers. In effect, an involved father conveys the message to his son that he understands that the boy is experiencing many confusing feelings about his mother, but that he needn't be afraid of such emotions. A father helps his son to appreciate that even when apart from his mother, he can still love and value her.

An important contribution is made to his son's individuation process when a father can help his son comprehend that people don't permanently vanish or die just because we separate from

them in order to become more of our own person. With the introduction of this momentous insight, a boy learns that he can say
good-bye to his mother when she ventures off, and yet gladly welcome her back and love her when she returns. In addition,
fathers help their boys to channel their feelings of separation
from their mothers elsewhere albeit in creative, sublimated
ways.

But boys whose parents have reestablished their spousal relationship grounded in their adult sexuality sustain yet another
loss at this time. They realize that not only are they different
from Mom, but that Mom and Dad have an exclusive relationship
in which they don't take part. In other words, the boy learns that
he is not in sole possession of either parent. What a blow to a
boy's natural sense of omnipotence to realize that he's not the
center of his parents' world!

Before, being loved was equated with being with the mother.
When fathers enter the picture, their sons enlarge the notion of
love and desire. The boy begins to understand that Mom loves
him and also loves Dad, just as Dad loves him and also loves
Mom. Thanks to his identification with his dad, he can say to
himself that his mom will love him as he becomes more of an
independent person because Dad is an independent person
whom she loves. This knowledge, that he can feel loved even if
momentarily excluded, is an important foundation for a boy to
carry into his future life. Similarly, a father can help his son hold
onto the feeling of being loved by his mother even when the boy
is feeling angry and hateful toward her.

For example, I recently observed three-year-old Roger climbing on the couch to drink his chocolate milk and then spilling it
all over the cushions. Irene, his mother, angrily yelled, "I told
you not to do that!" Roger felt sorry about what he did, but he
was particularly upset about his mother's reaction: as he later

voiced it to his father, "She looks like a witch!" Roger withdrew, refused to talk to her, and sat waiting for his father, Claude, to return from the store. When Claude walked in the door, Roger cried out, "Mommy's so mean to me! I hate her. You are so nice and never mean like she is!"

Luckily for Roger, both Irene and Claude understood that their son had to "split" his affection, turning his mother into the *bad* parent and his father into the *good* one. Claude's role, in this situation, is to hear and understand Roger's anxiety while at the same time supporting his wife. "Mommy is angry with you," he explained to his son, "because you didn't follow the rules about drinking milk on the couch. But she loves you very much and wants to help you learn to take care of things, just as do I." Thus, Roger stopped crying as he understood that he was still in his mother's good graces despite his mistake. Equally important, because Roger sees that he can't divide his parents by coming between them or turning them against each other, he feels reassured by the strength of their bond.

Boys who are able to weather this passage, from being center of the universe to one planet among others, emerge feeling as if they are loved even when they are excluded from other important relationships. Just as they learned what psychologists call "object permanence" a few months earlier, holding onto the thought of a person or object when neither is physically present, boys are now able to achieve "object constancy," feeling that "My mom and dad love me even when they are angry with me or when I am not with them."[5]

This is a major emotional development for the boy. It also marks an important cognitive leap in that Roger is learning to think more abstractly. To understand how this occurs, let's put the incident described above, about Roger spilling his milk, under a psychological microscope. Roger's first reaction is emotional: his mother gets mad at him, so he responds by worrying that she hates him. This is an automatic and primitive reaction; he doesn't have to think about it. We all respond to facial expressions and tone of voice on a gut level.

But Irene doesn't hate her son. At the moment, she feels angry and too upset to explain the complexity of her feelings. That's where Dad comes in. Because he's outside the situation, he's able to explain to Roger that although it seems as if his mom hates him, she really doesn't; she's simply upset about the spilt milk.

Dad's explanation not only validates and legitimizes Roger's feelings—by acknowledging that it was natural for Roger to think the way he did—but it also expands Roger's thinking by helping him to understand that his mother has her own internal experience of what's occurring and that it may differ considerably from what Roger more reflexively assumes. By clarifying and explaining Irene's reaction to Roger, Claude enables his son to feel heard and not blamed, which frees him to think about the situation in a new way. That is, because he doesn't feel threatened or attacked, Roger can carefully consider what his father said. He is learning that words can help him modulate, or temper his feelings.

In these ways, Roger is moving beyond the more automatic, reflexive phase, in which he merely responds to stimuli, into a realm in which he can think about what is happening for and to him, and ultimately, what others may be experiencing. This is a giant conceptual step forward, and will be reenacted many times in the future. What's important to recognize here is that fathers play a crucial role in encouraging conceptual and abstract thinking, helping their children to modulate, tame, and/or constructively channel their aggressive and sexual impulses, as well as more specifically difficult emotions such as anger, jealousy, and fear.

Interestingly, the success of this interaction between father and son depends significantly on the mother. She needs to recognize, accept, validate, and appreciate her partner's role in the triangle, as the "second other" in her child's life. Irene allowed her husband Claude to explain and interpret her feelings to their son. In essence, a mother's support of her child's father enables the child more consciously to begin recognizing the importance for him of the connection between his two parents.

A father, therefore, plays an essential role in helping his son ease his way through this transitional period. By guiding his son into the world while reclaiming his wife, he protects both wife and child from lingering too long in a fusional state. Accordingly, he directly facilitates the separation-individuation process that is so extremely important to a boy's long-term development. When fathers don't make their presence felt during this crucial developmental moment, however, boys feel the repercussions for their entire lives.

Phil's case is such an example. Although he was a successful lawyer, he was living a life of emotional poverty. He was in his late fifties and had been married and divorced three times, was estranged from his only sister, and lived an isolated existence except for an occasional trip to the stadium with one of his grown children. Moreover, he had engaged in a series of disassociated actions over the last decade that had resulted in his facing criminal charges and severing most of his professional and personal ties.

Through analysis, Phil's inner life was revealed as one where he felt dominated by a "Stone God." This omnipresent and putative "God" served to destroy his humanity by rendering human emotion and impulse as "evil." Utterly lacking in compassion, this primitive version of a young boy's misguided attempt to create an internal representation of a father to lead him was beset by difficulties. Such extremes in the male's conscience or superego commonly ensue when an undeveloped mind has no available, involved father (or surrogate) to help him form a more benevolent, yet realistic ideal. Thus, Phil's internal paternal image was described as a veritable "Moses or Abraham lying in the bushes waiting to sacrifice me for thoughts that violate the Ten Commandments." As a consequence, Phil's interior life was marked by persecutory anxiety, hopelessness, and guilt of dreaded proportion. His dreams frequently involved idealized figures who would righteously murder him for unspecified crimes.

The reconstruction of Phil's history showed that his father, a poor Eastern European immigrant who was seldom home in seeking to establish a life for his family in America, had not been able to recognize his small son as an independent "other" in his own right. This specific form of paternal absence ran concurrent with Phil, as a young boy, being virtually left to an exclusively feminine world comprising his aunt, grandmother, and sister, along with an invasive, depressed mother. No one was around to function as the secure other figure who might have provided Phil an introduction to the larger world.

Because of these circumstances, Phil's entry into that world was harsh. To protect himself, he developed narrow and rigid ideas about how he should live and how to evaluate himself. Without a father to model a more realistic and forgiving way of being a man, Phil created a version of maleness that was almost a caricature in that it did not allow him to have limits, weaknesses, or vulnerabilities. As a boy, Phil was also deprived of the opportunity to view his relationship with his mother from the outside. By incorporating his mother's limited perspective when he was too young to question it, he was unable to develop a full sense of his own humanity.

FATHERS AND SONS AT PLAY: THE MUTUAL BENEFITS

A father enters his son's consciousness not simply as a third person in the family, but as the person with whom the boy can most closely identify based on their physical similarities. This process of a son's "identification" with the father enables his son to develop his masculine identity and autonomy in a healthy manner and at an appropriate pace.

In particular, the father provides a model of masculinity that the boy can, in his own way, begin to emulate. Sons become enamored with their fathers especially during their second and third years, when they begin to imitate bathroom behavior, try on belts and hats that are too large for their small stomachs and heads, and assume a more mature tone of voice as they are learning to speak.

This male bonding, however, doesn't occur solely by means of a son *imitating* his father. By *playing* with their sons in more robust, physical ways, fathers introduce elements of excitement and discovery so that boys come away feeling as if the world of men includes pleasure, spontaneity, and vitality, not just the sharing of certain physical traits. This is certainly what Tom was able to give his son, Ian, in the playground—a sense of wonder, excitement, and adventure. Through essentially challenging their sons to try new things—through such seemingly simple measures as trying out the monkey bars at the playground or pounding the drums in the garage, for example—fathers gradually help their sons *differentiate*, which is a psychoanalytic way of saying that they develop into a separate, autonomous person with their own unique identities distinct from either parent. In these ways, fathers encourage their sons to explore what's beyond the safe and familiar.

Men carry memories of their fathers at this stage of their lives for their lifetimes. I've listened to many grown men near tears remembering how their fathers tickled them while tucking them in at night, wrestled with them on the living-room floor, and swam after them in a lake or pool pretending to be a shark. Edward, a patient of mine in his mid-thirties, never smiled as broadly as he did when recalling how his father used to stretch out next to him in bed when he was only three or four, and relate scary ghost stories which always ended with a tickle and a big kiss goodnight.

For my part, I can remember a game that I use to play with my son (as well as with my daughter) when he was very small. I would peek into his room and declare, "I'm going to get you . . . get you . . . get you!" He would get very excited, even playfully afraid, as he tried to crawl away from his fearsome dad. As I'd slowly overtake him, pick him up, and tickle him, he'd squeal with delight. Our game ended as we hugged one another, rolling over and over on the carpet. During his adolescence, we continued to play a version of this game—when he grabbed the keys to the car in an annoying teenage huff, I'd joke about how I'm "going to get you . . . get you . . ."

As fathers and sons create their special bond, they become a "team of two." Boys begin to understand what it means to be a man, to embrace their sense of masculinity and to feel comfortable in a male's body. Fathers who can engage with their sons in this way teach them to enjoy their bodies and man-to-man bodily contact without threat or danger. This rough-and-tumble play, as the research psychiatrist Allan Schore reports, helps sons to establish the necessary mental structures to govern their aggression and regulate violent expression.[6]

What many men do not realize is that while they are helping to guide their sons through this developmental period, their sons are likewise helping these fathers to expand upon their own notions of masculinity. I'll never forget a series of conversations I had with William, a wealthy businessman who had become a father relatively late in life. With death imminent, he wanted to reminisce about a pivotal moment in his relationship with his son, Bill, that he said transformed his life.

He explained to me that he had always been so driven to reach the top that having a child hadn't made him think twice about changing his daily habits. He thought nothing of staying at the office through dinner and not arriving home until seven or eight at night, long after Bill had gone to bed. When Bill turned three years old, however, something changed. "I began to enjoy playing with him," William told me. "He'd join me at breakfast and talk to me about silly little things as I drank my coffee, about how the sugar cube was really a car, and he'd take it on a journey, narrating his way around the kitchen table. Then he'd take the newspaper from me and pretend to read it, in a grown-up voice, making up stories that always made me laugh."

At about this same time, William realized that he was becoming restless in the office in the late afternoon. Instead of thinking about the important presentation he was about to make, he found himself thinking about spending time with Bill; suddenly, all he wanted to do was hurry home and play with him, "to teach him something new each day, to show him something that would take his breath away and leave him speechless." William then recalled wistfully, "I used to be that way, as a boy, full of wonder. I'd lost that capacity. And Bill was returning it to me."

Throughout the years of my practice, I have listened to many men like William—full-fledged denizens of the corporate world accustomed to fine hotels, four-star restaurants, and courtside seats at sporting events—rediscover the simple and unexpected pleasures of fatherhood. In the past, these men took the words from I Corinthians 13:11 to heart: "When I was a child, I spake as a child, I understood as a child, I thought as a child: when I became a man, I put away childish things." To "make it" in the world—to become a captain of industry, marry the right woman, climb the corporate ladder—these men thought they had to eschew, even repudiate, their softer and more childlike qualities. With their eye on the prize, they cultivated their ambitions, competitiveness, and self-assurance. They prided themselves on their ability to think in linear ways.

Children, however, don't think this way. They can spend countless hours building towers with blocks, want to hear the same stories over and over, and don't understand why they must take a bath every afternoon at five o'clock. Men who want to enter into a real relationship with their children realize that they need to rediscover and reclaim their more childlike qualities, the very ones they set aside in order to succeed in the outside world. By becoming more attuned to their children, they discover a back door into their *own* childhood, not through embracing childishness but by learning to value the qualities they'd abandoned in their quest for success. The sense of play, wonder, and curiosity, excitement and adventure, all come alive again for the father who engages with his child during these "magic" years.

Therefore, just as fathers help their sons learn that they can grow into boyhood and still stay connected to their mothers, sons are able to help their fathers recall and enjoy a more childlike way of experiencing themselves. Fathers who are able to achieve this often embrace a new way of being in the world. They become more physically demonstrative, for example, realizing that they can express their attachment to others, even other men, in ways that are physical but not sexual or competitive, much like the innocent ways in which children are physically affectionate with people they barely know. Sons also help their fathers broaden their sense of what it means to be a man. Allen, for example, was a brilliant and driven academician who relaxed by climbing mountains. From early on, he pushed and challenged his two sons toward both intellectual and athletic excellence. Evan, the older son, responded favorably to Allen's caring though demanding presence: he was a "straight A" student and star of the grade school's basketball and football teams.

Charlie, the younger son, had a rougher time. Not only was he chubby, but by age five, he was diagnosed with a learning disorder. Though he tried hard to be an athlete to please his father, his motor skills were lacking, so understandably he began to lose interest in sports in favor of embracing artistic and musical endeavors. Allen started to worry about Charlie, imagining him as someone who would ultimately be unable to "make it." "How can he get anywhere in this tough, competitive world without being bright and physically capable?" he wondered. "How can he possibly feel good about himself watching his brother do so well while he sits around drawing and fooling around with his clarinet? How is he even going to make a living?"

When Allen entered psychoanalytic therapy with me, I found myself particularly interested in his history as an only child who had lost his father at an early age and was raised by his mother who had never again dated. Through our work, Allen began to see how he had prematurely taken on the role of "man of the house," and how rigidly he'd come to define his masculinity as a result of feeling as if he had to grow up before he was ready. Eventually, he realized that he was projecting onto Charlie his own personal fears of not being sufficiently masculine.

With this understanding, Allen gradually was able to understand that being a man can take on a variety of forms, not just that of being brilliant or a strong athlete. Once he had established a newly restored relationship with his son, he told me that Charlie was "a good kid, who likes painting and may even grow up to be an artist . . . or perhaps not. What matters now is that I see who he is and that I encourage him to be himself in the best way he can." That Allen could voice these reflections about his son indicated, in addition to his expanded conception of manliness, his new comfort level in expressing his own softer side in ways he could not have before. In effect, Charlie unconsciously influenced his father to accept a part of himself he had always rejected.

DESIRE, AMBITION, AND ACHIEVEMENT

As boys gradually learn that they have separate, equally intense relationships with their fathers and mothers, they experience a kind of double mirror experience through which they discover their own sense of self. By evaluating these twin relationships, they gradually infer that they have a self that is independent of their parents. They experience themselves as people, or "subjects," who desire things, whether these things are material objects or actual people (namely, mother and father). If the father acts as a positive role model, boys can feel entitled to have such feelings of desire.[7]

A father also recognizes his son as a subject with his *own* desires. This allows the boy's sense of masculinity to develop further as he experiences himself as actively initiating and seeking the fulfillment of his needs. An example of this might be when a father comes home from work, sees his young son waiting eagerly at the door, and immediately greets him with a big hug. It seems like a simple interaction, but this subtle attunement of father and son is powerful: the boy wants the father to notice him, the father does, and they fulfill each other's wishes.

Furthermore, as boys gradually realize that their fathers have the ability to act independently in order to satisfy their own desires and needs in the larger world, they equate their fathers with independence, desire, and the ability to conquer obstacles to get what they want. This can often be observed in a playground scene, as the father encourages his son's excitement in trying out the monkey bars for the first time. The father notices and approves of his son's desire to explore new things and have new experiences, and the son perceives his father as powerful yet playful, a bridge to the outer world, rendering something that seems large and sometimes frightening more manageable.

Men whose fathers were unavailable during this crucial time often find themselves struggling with anxieties and fears pertaining to their desires and independence. Such was the case with Kevin, a successful professional in his early thirties, who came to see me because he found he could not enjoy anything. "I'm more neurotic than Woody Allen," he confided. He had been living with a woman for about five years, yet was tormented by obsessive doubts about the relationship, was unable to commit, and felt sexually removed.

As treatment progressed, Kevin's longing for his father to return and take him from his mother's influence and anxieties into a masculine world came into the light. He joyfully recalled his father's closeness when tucking him into bed as a small boy and playing "roughhouse" games together. At a certain point in his early childhood, however, his father withdrew from the family, and Kevin was left to be raised exclusively by his mother, who was so overprotective he was made afraid to go to so much as a baseball game for fear he'd get hit in the head with the ball and die. He also mentioned that his mother eventually protested the roughhouse games he engaged in with his father because she was afraid someone would get hurt. His father relented, and something Kevin found so much pleasure in went away, along with his father's ultimate departure from his life.

It was no wonder to me that Kevin grew up feeling aloof and unable to commit to a relationship. Whenever he experienced anything resembling physical desire or pleasure, he'd hear his mother's voice warning him of the danger and become frightened himself. Unfortunately, he feared everything outside of his mother's orbit but had had no father to intervene on his behalf, someone who could show him how these impulses might be modulated so that he could enjoy rather than fear them. His father could have "saved" Kevin from drowning in his mother's anxieties; instead, he failed to offer Kevin an escape route out of his intense engagement with his mother.

This pattern is not so unusual. When fathers don't sufficiently engage with their sons, these sons experience the regressive tug back to the more infantile desires associated with their mothers. However, if the father offers himself as a companion and model to his son, the intensity of the mother-son bond becomes mitigated as the boy's attention and interest shift to the outside world rather than the world in her arms. Moreover, as will become more apparent in the years ahead, an engaged father can help his son learn to balance his own desires with those of others.

COPING WITH LIMITS AND AUTHORITY

It's clear that fathers can significantly help their sons by modeling acceptable male behavior and by empathizing with their child's need to be recognized. But sometimes empathy isn't enough. Fathers also help their sons by bringing more of the outside world to bear on their sons' experiences, as Neil's case illustrates.

I worked with Neil just as his five-year-old son Sammy was resisting toilet training. Neil's own father had been very self-involved; in fact, most of Neil's memories of his father were ones in which his father had humiliated him. To his credit, Neil had vowed to treat his son differently, and as a result, when it came to his son's feelings, Neil was quite empathic—perhaps to the point of being excessive. Whenever the boy had an accident in his pants, Neil would say, "That's okay, you just need more time."

One day, Neil realized that this tactic wasn't working, and that his son needed something more than compassion to become toilet-trained. Unfortunately, Neil had no internal model of how to be an authoritative father without humiliating his son. I encouraged Neil to explore the ways in which he had unconsciously incorporated his father's attitudes (though behaving in what he considered the polar opposite of his father) and I worked with him to begin to construct a new internal sense of his own fatherly strength based on his long-standing desire to have a father's benevolent guidance and authority. In part by identifying with and internalizing my own non-demeaning manner of confronting Neil with his passivity, as well as by gaining insight into his unconscious tendency to reenact his father's behavior, he was able to "use" me to develop a healthy version of paternal authority.

The next time Sammy didn't make it to the bathroom in time, Neil said decisively, "Sam, that's enough of this. It's not okay for five-year-old boys to poop in their pants. It's not good for you. The other kids will start making fun of you, and they'll treat you as if you're a baby. I don't want you to have to go through that. I know this is scary for you, but I want to help you learn to handle this and you need to start now."

Neil wasn't sure how Sammy would react, but he was happily surprised. Sammy seemed to respond positively to his father's strength, to his ability to set limits, to delineate what was acceptable and what was not. Just a few days later, Neil left a happy message on my voice mail announcing that Sammy had finally gotten it right.

This is a classic example of a man who tried so hard *not* to be like his own father that he overcompensated, erring too far in the opposite direction. Yes, young boys need empathy from their fathers, but they also need their fathers' authoritative guidance and limit setting in order to take the next developmental step of negotiating in the world. For Sammy, an understanding of his feelings was important, but it wasn't enough. Neil's fatherly task was not simply to communicate his compassion for his son, but to recognize that his son needed a significant push.

But just as Neil was able to help Sammy take the next developmental step, he was simultaneously learning something from remaining engaged with his son: a person can be assertive and authoritative, even insistent, without being humiliating. Because of his unhappy experiences with his own father, he'd never been able to distinguish between being *overbearingly* authoritarian and *constructively* authoritative. By learning to become appropriately authoritative in order to help his son, Neil was able to incorporate this new behavior into his personality, giving him a fuller sense of his own masculine identity.

Engaged fathers teach their sons—and are taught by their sons— to see the world less in terms of black and white and more in shades of gray. Sons learn that they can experience different types of relationships and handle the feelings these relationships evoke, while fathers learn that the realms of achievement and relationships are neither mutually exclusive nor opposite poles in a binary world.

The bond created between father and son during these years, which is so mutually healing and beneficial, will soon be tested. If early childhood is about discovering intense feelings, then the next phase is about learning to take control of these feelings. Fathers help their sons regulate their emotions while boys help their fathers deal with the thorny issues of competition and rivalry. The stronger the early bond between fathers and sons, the easier the next few years may prove.

4

GUIDING BOYS TOWARD THE WORLD OF MEN

Train a lad in the way he ought to go;
He will not swerve from it even in old age.

—PROVERBS 22:6[1]

Closeness and competitiveness are the hallmarks of the phase of development Sigmund Freud termed the "oedipal stage," when boys are between the ages of three and a half to nearly six. Although boys look to their fathers for guidance, they also lock horns over important issues of autonomy and achievement. When these conflicts between fathers and sons are successfully negotiated, sons learn to deal constructively with their aggression, competitive feelings, and exploratory desires as they further their healthy sense of masculinity.

In this chapter, I will discuss how fathers can help their sons to successfully navigate in the world of men and how the ways in which they "lock horns" with one another set them on course for the kinds of relationships they will have with people in the world outside their family. This father-son struggle can play out in many ways. One example is Marty, a patient of mine, and his five-year-old son, Jason.

Marty told me about something that was bothering him. He described sitting with Jason building with Legos and noticing how much he enjoyed building next to his son; then he spontaneously said to Jason, "Hey, my tower is getting to be pretty tall."

Jason replied that his tower was "much, much bigger" than his father's and as his competitive juices began to flow, he grabbed another handful of blocks, adding them to his tower until it started to wobble and finally crashed to the floor. Jason then began to cry.

Marty, who was pleased with his own, much more secure tower, took a moment to comfort Jason, and help him to rebuild his fallen tower. Marty then tried to instruct his son about providing more support to the tower's base, but Jason wasn't interested. He wanted to do it his way, and so he set about building a second tower the same way he'd built the first, by adding brick after brick to the top.

Jason proudly boasted that his tower was now taller than his father's just seconds before it crumbled to the floor like the last one. Even more enraged and humiliated than before, Jason burst into tears.

Marty confided in me that he had wanted to tell Jason, "I told you so!" though he wisely refrained. But he wasn't sure what to do and asked me, "What *should* I have said? And what am I supposed to do with that feeling in the pit of my stomach that I can't squelch where I realize I'm more than a little happy to see my own tower still standing while my son's lies in ruins?" He finally did tell his son that he may want to start building it again; but Jason would have none of it as he stormed out of the room, saying, "Leave me alone!"

This vignette, ripe with oedipal undertones, suggests the importance of a father's recognition of his own competitive feelings with his son. As I'll elaborate later in the chapter, it is crucial that fathers learn to use their aggression in constructive ways, particularly because a father's primary role during these oedipal years is to mentor and securely guide his son into the world of men. Fathers are especially needed because around the time their sons turn three, boys begin to acknowledge the painful reality: that as close as they may feel to their mothers, they are *not* like their mothers physically or biologically. This news is not only a blow; it forces a boy to alter his perception of himself. In conjunction with this narcissistically wounding realization, between their third and fourth birthdays, boys are simultaneously undergoing an intense period of pulling away, both physically and emotionally, from the mother with whom they had been so close. This effort to differentiate themselves from their mothers, as described by many developmentally oriented psychoanalysts, can be perplexing, frightening, and saddening, as well as exciting and challenging.[2] Boys instinctively turn to their fathers for help in negotiating such an important transition.

FATHERS MODEL A MALE IDENTITY

An engaged father empathizes with his son's need to move away from his mother while simultaneously offering a healthy alternative love object: himself. A major part of successfully showing his son the value of embracing this new relationship is by making obvious the similarities inherent in being male, which ultimately helps the boy slowly grasp a healthy sense of *his* gender identity. For example, even though many boys learn to use the toilet at an earlier age, only now do they begin feeling pride (and pleasure) during the experience of urinating while standing. They also recognize that they are doing something their fathers can do while their mothers, quite obviously, cannot. This new skill enables them to focus on being more like Dad rather than on "pleasing Mommy." Furthermore, when the father presents himself as a male model of bathroom behavior—which includes, in addition to urinating standing up, shaving his face—the boy can absorb the elements that make adult males unique. Differentiating himself from his mother and the so-called "feminine" is thereby further encouraged, core gender identity is supported, and phallic masculinity and gender role are better established.

Fathers teach their sons to "piss in the wind," "make bubbles" in the toilet, and otherwise enjoy the touch, familiarity, and control afforded by aiming their penis like a newfound toy. The capacity for ingenuity and pleasure in autonomous mastery is new. It is something they did not experience so straightforwardly when they were younger, but now it is directly reinforced as they proudly display their phallic power in their fathers' presence. This healthy exhibitionism and accompanying phallic omnipotence express the boy's intensely felt need for his father's admiration and reciprocal identification.[3] Moreover, the privacy reminiscent of the bond boys had with their mothers becomes less important as the male model of peeing together takes precedence. This signals the beginning of a boy's enjoyment of male bonding.

I'll never forget taking my son, Alex, when he was about four, to an NBA basketball game in Los Angeles. During one of our several trips to the bathroom, Alex found himself standing next to one of the city's sports heroes, Darryl Strawberry, who was then playing baseball for the L.A. Dodgers. Alex stared at him—I think he was flabbergasted merely to be standing beside a man so tall (Darryl is about six foot seven). And then he said to the Straw, "I can hit the bull's-eye, can you?" Strawberry broke out in a smile so warm that he will forever remain dear to me for his kind acknowledgment of my son's achievement.

The mutual interest in each other's bodies, however, extends beyond the bathroom. It's evident when father and son rough-house on the floor or stage an arm-wrestling tournament. This robust, constructively aggressive and sensual physicality (along with a sense of play, excitement, and discovery) all help to assure the son that the world of men includes pleasure, spontaneity, and vitality. When fathers and sons are able to enjoy affectionate body contact, typically involving large muscle activity, boys imitate their fathers and, in turn, deepen their masculine identification. Through such "rough-and-tumble" play, boys directly experience their fathers' controlled yet authoritative masculine strength, and learn to use aggression constructively. In short, a boy embarks on forming his initial sense of masculinity largely by identifying with his father's physicality, modulated aggression, autonomy, and eagerness to explore.

REDEFINING MASCULINITY WHEN DIFFERENTIATING FROM THE MOTHER

By creating a safety zone in which boys can express their autonomy, curiosity, and aggression, fathers pass on to their sons another lesson: that masculinity also has a soft, nurturing, and protective side. Previously, boys associated these caring qualities with their mothers; but now, as boys realize that their dads take care of them as well, they recognize that affection and caretaking are not exclusively feminine qualities. And in recognizing his father as a loving man, the boy himself can love in conflict-free ways as well since he has already embraced the similarities between them. Instead of renouncing all of his "soft" qualities, he can hold onto these traits and still think of himself as a "man" like his father because he no longer associates them solely with his mother.

The father also acts as a moderating influence on his son, encouraging the boy to move away from an all or nothing position about the so-called feminine parts of himself. Boys with this insight develop a conception of their masculinity that is not rigid or fixed but varied; their sense of maleness isn't an either/or proposition, but rather a complex mixture of multiple identifications with both parents. In time, boys learn to acknowledge and accept the loss of the close bond to their mothers while also realizing that their sense of masculinity isn't something fragile or brittle, but instead quite flexible, and secure. Such a boy should grow up to be a man who is comfortable with a more fluid, and thereby more healthy, sense of masculinity.

As a result, the son is able to wean himself from his mother in a way that is gradual rather than abrupt, effortless instead of traumatic, and partial instead of total, because he does not perceive masculinity and femininity as being so disparate or at opposite ends of the spectrum. When he can integrate qualities from both his mother and his father while simultaneously recognizing that he is an autonomous being, who is not identified so strongly or exclusively with either parent, a boy can differentiate himself from his mother more naturally.

·   ·   ·

THE SIGNIFICANCE OF A FATHER'S INVOLVED
PRESENCE IN CULTIVATING HEALTHY MASCULINITY

For boys on their journeys to becoming men, gender identity and constancy are difficult to achieve. This is because as a boy grows, he receives powerful messages, both from within the family and from the outside world, that he has to stop identifying with his mother. Indeed, he is urged to separate from her, often prematurely, as well as to display behaviors that are specifically not associated with mothers or femininity in general. To experience themselves as masculine, boys are pressured to repudiate any and all aspects of themselves that might be construed as womanly. They also learn to anticipate strong negative reactions for cross-gender behavior and attitudes from their parents, peers, and society-at-large any time they cross certain gender boundaries.[4]

A boy who doesn't "cut the apron strings" is berated as a "mama's boy" or a "sissy." Our culture uses shame to ensure that boys leave their mothers and all female behavior behind once they reach a certain age. Boys may grow up particularly sensitive to shame as a result of being humiliated, often brutally, for behaving "like a girl." Because the opprobrium for this type of behavior is directed at them when they are so young, and because of its vehemence, boys want only to escape from shame. To do this, they create rigid boundaries between masculine and feminine behaviors. With these in place, they won't risk exposing themselves to more shame.

Yet most boys also want to recapture and preserve positive aspects of their earliest nurturing relationship with their mothers even as they know these feelings have to be disavowed. As a result, boys and men are left with a longing for something that had once been present in their lives but can no longer be consciously embraced. This is why so many men are insecure about their masculinity and, to compensate, why they expend so much energy affirming it. Inside, sensing how they really feel, they worry that they're not real men.

Psychoanalysts refer to the rigid, exaggerated adherence to a stereotype of masculine behavior sought by many boys, and later, men, as "phallicism." The phallus, represented by the boy's penis, is actually a mythic, archetypal monolith or talisman that, because it is permanently erect and available, stands for invulnerability, freedom from dependency, strength, untrammeled growth, and masculine omnipotence. It will shield the boy from experiencing loss—particularly loss of the closeness with his mother. That's because the boy imagines that his penis can conquer the world, including his mother, and will never be viewed as needy or weak.[5]

While this type of phallic narcissism is a natural, or adaptive, stage in every boy's development, it remains a primitive response that does not serve a boy well as he matures. The boy who has "good enough" parents—a mother who recognizes and supports her son's maleness, and an involved, responsive father—finds that the dominance of his phallic narcissism naturally wanes. In its place, a more integrated sense of maleness begins to evolve. When a boy's phallicism does *not* diminish, often because no father is present to help him during his early individuation attempts, the boy develops a rigid sense of masculinity that leaves him unable to admit to weakness, fallibility, or dependence. He remains stuck in his phallic narcissism and frequently will have considerable trouble forming intimate relationships.

A more inclusive conception of a boy's masculinity, one that I contend ideally integrates both masculine and feminine qualities, evolves when several factors are in place. First, a young boy needs a father who is involved with and available to his son, shepherding the boy through his development. This father also must be one who respects women and femininity, as well as his son's unique way of being himself. Optimally, such fathers are sufficiently secure in their own manhood to be nurturing and sensitive, as well as authoritative and mentoring, toward their sons.

To support their son's masculine identification, both parents need to recognize and accept the "otherness" of their partner. If fathers don't hate or fear women and mothers don't hate or fear men, and if competitive feelings can be tolerated in the context of a fundamentally supportive family, then a boy won't feel compelled to side with either Mom or Dad, thereby emotionally splitting himself apart in the process. Such a boy won't feel pressured to abruptly and dramatically cut his ties to his mother, repudiating his attachment to her along the way. Instead, he'll realize that he can extend those apron strings so they become more like a secure, yet flexible elastic band—a powerful symbol of protection and shelter—as he reaches out to his father, who will guide him through the world of men. In this way, an involved father both facilitates and buffers this transition: the more the father is secure in his own sense of maleness, the more he will be able to help his son make the transition from maternal safety to paternal identification.[6]

For an involved and loving father, his *gender role identity*, particularly when reflecting nurturing and caretaking qualities that society may characterize as feminine, won't threaten his *core gender identity* as a man. Such a man doesn't need to think of himself as more masculine when he is being authoritative, aggressive, dominant, or independent; neither does he have to be "all man" to feel manly. Rather, he can accept both the limits of his gender and the fact that masculine gender is inclusive.

When a boy does not benefit from good enough fathering during this period, whether the father is absent or simply unavailable to help his son in constructive ways, this boy might have extreme difficulties later on in his life, as is illustrated by Seth's case. Seth was a rock guitarist and, on the surface, appeared very much a "man"; however, he carried a deeply rooted sense of shame for some reason, and told me he had considered himself a "sissy" since the age of five. As a result, he persisted in defensive phallicism that involved repudiating his emotional self through an exaggerated yet aloof, "cool" masculine demeanor.

Seth was an only child, whose parents divorced when he was seven years old. His highly narcissistic father was contemptuous of all women while also prone to tantrums and impulsive behavior. He had subsequently remarried twice, and had carried on extramarital affairs throughout these marriages, yet he would constantly caution Seth to be careful because "all women are out to use men." His mother, on the other hand, was described as "very doting." Seth went on to tell me that she didn't like it when he had girlfriends, and discouraged him from learning to drive until he was twenty. He also mentioned that he had recently discovered that she had breast-fed him well past his third birthday. Additionally, much like Seth's father, she was highly critical of her former spouse and of men in general.

Now, Seth found himself desperately seeking a "father figure" who could help him discover who he "really was" and assist him to feel, in his own words, "okay to be who I really am." During our early sessions, he felt lost. Sometimes a little boy, sometimes a young teenager desperately in need of direction, he seemed as if he were in a state of arrested development, coming to me not to explore his troubles but rather for a "feeding"; that is, he required little from me other than to be present and exclusively attentive to him. He came to our sessions every week without fail, and ultimately I found myself acting as the father figure he had been looking for: a kind and loving mentor, who could direct him toward an informed understanding of both himself and the world around him.

Seth often spoke about his feelings of inferiority and shame, which revolved around his masculinity, specifically that he constantly experienced an overwhelming desire to "hide" what he called his "emotional self" in "a dark cave" every time he felt himself indulging in any "weak and feminine" behaviors. The cave alluded to a place where he'd hidden his emotional or feminine self, and the fact that it was dark spoke to both the depth and the terror of his early bodily identification with his mother.

During his third year of treatment, Seth described a dream in which he saw a piano in a friend's house. He began playing it, started to cry uncontrollably, and felt exceptionally sad. He became embarrassed and tried to leave the room without anyone seeing him, but he ultimately could neither hide his feelings nor leave the room.

Following the retelling of his dream, we were able to explore Seth's "repulsion" at the thought of touching his mother, as well as his long-standing terror of "feminine" women. These sentiments certainly arose from his inability to connect with his father at the crucial period in his development when society expects young boys to pull away from their mothers. Seth's mother was holding onto Seth too tightly, and with no father figure to help loosen her grasp, Seth was left with no other option than to be held, much to his reluctance. We also used this dream as an outlet to discuss how, without an available and mature father, Seth grew up feeling stranded. He had no healthy, adult man to identify with, and he was at a loss to understand how he could find maleness by relating to his mother. As a result, Seth created for himself a rigid version of masculinity, an either/or gender identity wherein he was either masculine *or* feminine, either strong and independent *or* weak and clingy. According to this schema, he had no choice but to repudiate "feminine" qualities in order to feel like a man.

An indispensable component of what I did for Seth was to become a model for a full, all-encompassing masculinity with both paternal and maternal qualities. This helped him to understand that his narrowly constructed sense of masculinity left him estranged from himself and others. By exploring his conflicts around his sense of masculinity, and the underlying unconscious restrictions that he had placed upon himself in order to adapt to his earlier familial circumstances, Seth was able to use his insights to negotiate an internal cease-fire. No longer at war within, he could realize that both his masculine and feminine sides were available rather than forbidden. He saw that a healthy, stable, fluid, and flexible sense of masculinity is founded on a dialogue between our masculine and feminine sides, and that acknowledging this ongoing dialogue is the only way a man can remain true to himself in all his diversity, complexity, and multiplicity.

FATHERS AND SONS COMPETING:
FACING THE OEDIPAL CHALLENGE

By the time boys begin kindergarten, preferably with their initial sense of masculinity sufficiently established as a result of having had good enough fathers guiding them, they are confronted with a new challenge, commonly referred to as the "oedipal conflict."

This key developmental stage is named for King Oedipus, whose tragic story is recounted by Sophocles, one of the great Greek dramatists, in the play *Oedipus Rex*. According to the most straightforward and well-known rendering of the legend,

Laius, the king of Thebes, was informed by an oracle that his newborn son, Oedipus, would grow up to murder his father and marry his mother. Hoping to avert this tragedy, Laius ordered that the infant be exposed to die on a mountainside. By chance, a shepherd found the infant and brought him to Corinth, where he was raised in the royal family.

When Oedipus was a young man, he heard the oracle predicting his father's death at his own hand. To prevent this, he immediately fled Corinth for Thebes, still under the impression that his adopted parents were his biological parents. At a crossroads, he met a man with whom he got into an argument about the right-of-way, and Oedipus impulsively slew him, unaware that this man was in fact his father. Making his way to Thebes, Oedipus solved a riddle and relieved the city of its plague, and the grateful Thebans made him their king because Laius had just been killed. As a reward, he was given for a wife Queen Jocasta, the late Laius' wife and Oedipus' own biological mother.

Years later, furious that Oedipus is tampering with his fate, the gods visit Thebes with yet another plague. Oedipus is then told that only when the murderer of Laius is discovered will the plague be lifted, so he vows to find the truth. Ultimately, he learns that he is in fact the murderer, not to mention the husband of his own mother with whom he has had a number of children. Beyond despair, Jocasta hangs herself and Oedipus gouges out his eyes with Jocasta's brooch. Though he has tried to escape his destiny, he has fallen squarely into its net, and is in fact the agent of his own downfall.

Two millennia after Sophocles, Sigmund Freud referred to this legend to illuminate the psychological phenomenon he appropriately called the "Oedipus complex." During this period of development, Freud proposed, a boy's fantasies shift from being his mother's baby to her lover, and from his father's baby to his competitor. In other words, father, mother, and son enter into a triangular relationship characterized by desire, competition, jealousy, rejection, and aggression. Most significant from the Freudian viewpoint is the fact that young boys, as if drunk with their newfound masculinity, enter into a period of rivalry with their fathers, often competing for their mothers' attention.

What happens is that the boy's traumatic loss of what felt like paradise—his symbiotic closeness with his mother early in his life—leaves him feeling as if he needs to become powerful enough to defeat the forces that are keeping her from him now. His unconscious wish to regain that lost sense of unity with her typically takes the form of a wish to conquer and possess her, to penetrate her and to have her all to himself. This is an example of "phallic power": a boy's illusion that sheer willpower can transcend limitations. Specifically, the son thinks he can win over his mother and replace his father.

But no sooner does a boy enjoy this nascent sense of masculine power than he begins to fear losing it to what he now perceives as his rival, his "vengeful" father. The boy's overblown sense of strength leaves him feeling terrified that his much stronger father will read his mind, uncover the boy's secret desires, and, seeking revenge for the boy's fantasies, retaliate. The ultimate retaliation would be for the father to castrate his son, rendering the boy not only powerless but sexless. This is what is known as "castration anxiety," which is manifest in fears of loss of love, punishment, and humiliation from the father, as well as in the loss of capacity to feel desire itself.

To keep himself safe from being overwhelmed by his fears of reprisal and competitive impulses toward his father, a boy has to learn to channel these impulses. Once again, he turns to his father. But his father, interestingly enough, is likely to be experiencing the same feelings of rivalry, anger, and aggression toward his son. No matter how old a man may be, he is not above such feelings. The Oedipus story, for instance, isn't simply about a boy killing his father and marrying his mother, as Freud and the early psychoanalytic thinkers interpreted it; it's also about Laius' excessive pride in trespassing against the gods, and his intention to kill his son. In fact, many contemporary psychoanalysts focus not so much on Oedipus but rather on Laius as representing the darker side of fatherhood.[7]

A father helps his son during this period by recognizing and then taming his own competitive impulses so that he can once again exist as a positive role model for the boy. Even in the context of competition and rivalry, a father who is able to feel proud and encourage his son's budding sense of aggressive strength can demonstrate the genuineness of his love and help soothe the angry sentiments his son is unavoidably experiencing.

A good example of this occurred in the case of my patient Marty, and his son Jason, discussed at the beginning of the chapter. Hours after Jason had stormed out of the room following the collapse of his tower, Marty noticed that Jason had also kicked down and scattered his father's tower in pieces. Marty felt enraged and began cursing loudly, only to realize that he had to find a way to modulate his temper. He knocked on Jason's door: seeing his son cowering under the covers, he realized that the boy was afraid of him and felt powerless.

As angry as Marty was, he did not wish to humiliate Jason or to encourage him to avoid responsibility for his own actions. Using his understanding of Jason's competitive impulses and fears toward his much bigger father, Marty calmly but firmly sat down on the bed and told Jason that what he did was not all right and that if he destroyed someone else's efforts, he had better "pick up the pieces." Before kissing his son and saying goodnight, Marty told Jason that he understood how much he wanted to make the "biggest tower," but that sometimes he won't be able to do so and he'll have to learn to deal better with his disappointment.

If the father isn't available to his son during this phase, the boy can be plagued with jealousy and feelings of exclusion as an adult. Dave, for example, came to see me in his middle forties because he'd been feeling increasingly irritable at home. Describing himself as a "jealous type," he complained about how much time his wife spent talking on the telephone with her friends, helping their fourteen-year-old son with his academic work, or shopping with their seventeen-year-old daughter. Inevitably, Dave felt left out, snubbed and ignored.

As we discovered together over the course of his therapy, his parents' marriage had been so entangled that it apparently left no room for the children. As a child, Dave's perception of his parents' seemingly exclusive relationship left him feeling as if he had to fight to win the attention of others. This extended into his adult relationships, which were all seen as similar competitions for attention. Because Dave's father couldn't reach out to him when he was small, particularly during the oedipal phase, Dave the adult found himself perpetually excluded, trapped in a competitive oedipal struggle, trying to "win" the person he desired from rivals—he had even reached the point where he experienced his own children as bitter opponents. Fortunately, once Dave became aware of his problem, he no longer needed to live it out so unconsciously and painfully in his present-day relationships.

The oedipal father must be able to "hate" others, but particularly his son, in a contained manner. The pederastic Laius represents the outcome of unconscious, intergenerational rivalry enacted by a malevolent, vindictive father. Loving fathers must also know their own envy of and competitiveness toward their sons and sublimate their darker impulses by making efforts directed toward limit setting and age-appropriate differentiation. Through this boundary structuring, fathers promote healthy identification, superego development, and the capacity to accept and tolerate aggression, conflict, and ambivalence. The good enough oedipal father is thereby established as a figure of benign authority. This, in turn, greatly reduces the chances that he will act like King Laius.

It is not always easy, however, for a father to walk the fine line between competing too hard or too little with his son. Boys at this age especially need their father's strength, and to experience healthy male aggression in order to feel comfortable with their own. However, some fathers can't control their competitive aggression. Pat Conroy's novel *The Great Santini* portrays the disastrous consequences of such a father, who wasn't able to get over the need to "slaughter" his son, thereby destroying his boy's self-esteem and sense of self-worth in the process.[8]

In order for the son to take in and accept his father's male strength, the father needs to compete in a modulated, orderly fashion. He needs to relinquish his wish to dominate his son. But should a father always win? Or should he sometimes let his son win? There's no way to answer such a question. What a father needs to do is watch his son and see how he reacts to victory and defeat. The goal is to push and challenge the boy, not to overwhelm him.

Boys whose fathers don't challenge their sons' nascent sense of power in a restrained manner often have difficulties forming close relationships when they're older, and consequently, grow up with a specific form of father hunger. Such was the case with Raymond, a man in his mid-thirties who began treatment following an incident of physically abusing his wife. He was depressed, remorseful, and feared destroying his marriage "with the best woman [he had] ever known." Moreover, occasional episodes of alcohol and drug abuse threatened his career, causing him to worry that, like his father, he'd "make shit out of everything worthwhile."

His alcoholic father had abandoned Raymond and his infant twin brothers to his "loving but very doting" mother's care when he was six years old. Through he "hung out with many coworkers," Raymond had enormous difficulty relying on other men unless they were joined together to "defeat another organization." A charming veneer barely disguised the considerable distrust that initially marked his relationship with me. I sensed that his being an African-American man made it difficult for him to feel safe with me in what he might experience as a competitive context. Once I was able to introduce our racial differences and his concerns about me as a white man as topics for discussion, Raymond saw that I was open to learning from him and also that I would speak truthfully to him. In short, by creating a context in which he could begin to talk safely about "sensitive" topics such as our cultural differences, Raymond was eventually able to use me as a father surrogate to help him with his rather arrested differentiation process. Our work now could begin to explore Raymond's deeper transferences and dynamics reflecting his sense of oedipal conquest and the accompanying failure to establish triangular relations. These dynamics are encapsulated by what Raymond said in describing his mother: "She was like my wife in a way, and I was her 'special dude,' who helped her raise the twins."

During our second year of working together, Raymond related a dream that reflected his longing for a mature and responsible father who would be connected to his mother. This *triadic father* would be emotionally involved both with Raymond and his mother, while also being someone with whom he could identify and yet remain junior to. In the dream, Raymond was a teenager playing one-on-one basketball on his driveway with his much-revered high school coach. In the midst of an intense game, Raymond elbowed the older man away. The coach's nose bloodied and he dropped to the ground like a "wounded bear," leaving Raymond stunned and frightened.

His mother had been watching and she ran straight to the bleeding coach, ministering to him. She looked toward Raymond as if to say, "I love your teacher like a husband and I will take care of him even if you are scared."

Raymond awoke feeling upset yet oddly relieved. To me, his relief spoke eloquently of his longing for a father with whom he could identify while still remaining young. In psychological terms, he was searching for a strong oedipal father who, being *coupled with* his mother, would be able to take over the burdens of fatherhood. This would release Raymond from feeling plagued by the unconscious burden of acting as a "child-father," with its accompanying sense of oedipal victory and excessive guilt. As we discussed this dream, Raymond was able to acknowledge his dependence on me as a man whom he needed to validate his private experience and respect his vulnerability. He needed me to be a transference father who could both bear his distrust and understand the competitive and aggressive feelings that had come alive in our relationship. As a result of this work, he began to voice his criticisms and negative feelings toward me more freely, and because I encouraged him to do so, he realized that his expression of those feelings wouldn't defeat me or destroy our relationship.

With this understanding, he was able to overcome some of his trust issues and begin to build some real friendships with other men. Most significantly, he was beginning to understand that his sons needed him to use his authority to help them develop, rather than disappearing and leaving their development solely in the hands of his wife and their school. Raymond continued to require my help in learning to channel his aggression and use his authority constructively. Over time, he was better able to express himself in words, especially with his wife and sons, while proudly becoming more active in raising his boys.

But a father need not be physically absent from the home for his son to grow up with a father hunger that makes it difficult for the son, in turn, to father his own son. As this chapter has shown, sons need their fathers as authority figures who can socialize them for the "real" world. Many fathers, like Raymond, have to learn how to teach and discipline their sons with calm yet unyielding authority. When fathers can accomplish this, their sons emerge from this developmental period thinking of their fathers as compassionate and benevolent, yet authoritative. Moreover, by serving as a civilizing, authoritative presence for his son, a father has a unique opportunity to resolve some of his own issues with authority. Oftentimes, these long-standing issues, which arose in the context of the person's past relationship with his own father, have a tendency to spill over to people and settings outside the home—at work, for instance, or whenever men interact with an authority figure.

What all boys wish for is a father who can shelter them with what the psychologist and author Sam Osherson describes as "male strength."[9] This strength shows sons how to become strong men without also becoming destructive, which in turn enables the sons to facilitate their fathers' development during this stage of life, and beyond.

5

ENCOURAGING MASTERY, COMPETENCE, AND PRIDE IN MIDDLE CHILDHOOD

Teach your children well . . .
And feed them on your dreams.

—CROSBY, STILLS, NASH, AND YOUNG[1]

Between the ages of six and twelve, children mature very rapidly, undergoing enormous changes in terms of their moral, physical, social, and especially their cognitive development. As their brains mature and become more complex, they are capable of higher-level mental thought; they eschew associative, magical thought for a more cause-and-effect, reality-based way of thinking. In psychoanalytic language, the growing boy seeks to "sublimate" his impulses—the very ones that earlier in childhood may have led him to dream, imagine expansively, and play—by expressing them more indirectly through creative hobbies and industrious activities.

At this stage, boys are also striving to be purposeful and productive in order to win their fathers' recognition and approval. Instead of trying to outdo their fathers, as they did a few years earlier during the oedipal phase, boys focus more on what their dads can do, recognizing they are forces in the larger world. Eager to emulate their dads, they even develop special interests and skills that mirror those of their fathers.

Sigmund Freud called this the "latency period," referring to the fact that the intense sexual and aggressive feelings that predominated during the preceding oedipal phase have now become more dormant, or latent.[2] It's almost as if they have retreated underground, only to reemerge when the "stormy" days of puberty begin. In other words, middle childhood represents a type of sexual moratorium.

This is not a period of quiet emotions, however; in fact, the inner lives of boys at this age are often filled with a great deal of emotional commotion. Moreover, because their feelings are sometimes so concentrated and difficult to regulate, boys do best when they can turn to their fathers to learn how to effectively deal with the intensity of their conflicting sentiments while simultaneously negotiating the outside world. It is not surprising that elementary school–age boys with closely involved fathers do show a greater capacity for empathy, increased self-esteem, and a lower incidence of depression, as well as more flexible attitudes about gender and life in general.[3]

· · ·

FURTHER INITIATING AND MENTORING SONS INTO THE "WORLD OF MEN"

The process whereby a father initiates and mentors his son in how to behave in groups begins years earlier, when father and son first become companions. At first, the father drew his toddler-aged son out of his exclusive orbit with the mother. A few years later, during the oedipal period, the process intensified as Dad showed his son how to modulate his feelings toward both his mother and father. Now, during middle childhood, a father introduces his latency-age son to the pleasures of communal play and achievement by joining with him in organized activities, often team sports led either by dads themselves or by coaches who serve as father surrogates. These types of activities also offer boys important outlets for their competitive and aggressive strivings, as well as for their affection.

Latency-age boys tend to flock together, creating an environment without girls. It's not at all uncommon for boys this age to suddenly drop their friendships with girls, for while it was perfectly acceptable and appealing to play together a few years ago, now even acknowledging a member of the opposite sex can threaten a boy's nascent sense of masculinity. This segregation furthers male identification and mastery while simultaneously further distancing boys not only from their mothers but from all that females represent. Turning their backs on the female, boys undergo a ritual passage into the world where men's connections to each other are obvious and unabashedly acknowledged, a place where they can experience an intense sense of belonging.

When fathers introduce their sons into the world of team sports and other group activities, explains the psychologist William Pollack, boys learn to transform their male aggression into healthy competition and even love and intimacy.[4] They not only learn about satisfying their needs for achievement, competition, and mastery, but they also learn to submerge their own needs to those of the larger group. Though boys actively provoke competition within the team, constantly asking each other "who has the best swing?" for example, they learn to tease one another in a joking tone of voice, without real hostility or rancor. They come to appreciate that competition can exist in a context of cooperation. By following their fathers' lead, boys see that they can transform their impulses into acceptable, socialized behavior in order to get along with others.

Fathers are also needed as mentors for these groups of boys to help them channel their instinctual impulses into social behavior. Identification with these mentoring men helps to provide new outlets for the instinctual demands that boys experience. Both communal play and more spontaneous, expressive forms of masculinity develop through this fatherly involvement. The virtues of mastering fear and pain, as well as pleasurable experiences often marked by tenderness, accumulate as mentored boys establish an internal brake on their aggressive and sexual impulses, combining these impulses into new behavioral forms, which are frequently manifested in playfulness, empathy, and intimacy.

Fathers tend to "coach" their sons to overcome their fears and pains in gender-specific ways. For example, a friend whose son plays football described a game during which his son fell to the ground after a crunching block. "The second he didn't get up," my friend explained, "my wife became terrified and said, 'He has to come out of the game.'" In contrast, my friend described how he just watched the coach run out to the boy, and after a few more seconds, observed their son sitting up, somewhat dazed but apparently fine. The boy walked to the sidelines and both parents went down to talk to him. My friend's wife asked the boy if he wanted to go home, while the father said to him, "Listen, sit on the bench for a minute, and when the coach thinks you're ready, go back in. You're okay, I can tell." The son smiled at both of them, and in a few minutes went back into the game.

The reactions of either parent in these gender-typed ways can be helpful or problematic, particularly when taken to the extreme. We see such extremes, for example, when a father persuades his son to ignore his pain altogether. In this way, the father teaches his son to disregard pain's signal function, which can put the boy at risk for incurring more serious injury. It's not surprising that husbands and wives often have such different reactions. Although significant societal changes are occurring as girls are introduced to competitive sports early on, many women, particularly in past generations, haven't been socialized as men were to take pride in tolerating pain and learning to "hang tough." This point was underscored in the famous scene in the movie *A League of Their Own* when the manager (played by Tom Hanks) admonishes one of his female baseball players who begins to cry after doing poorly: "There's no crying in baseball."

During this period, boys also learn to negotiate a paradox: how to become part of a group and yet to begin the process of separating themselves from the peer pressure of the group. This is a difficult task because boys this age are particularly vulnerable to peer pressure. They want to go along with the majority even if they perceive an action as wrong. Thus, boys look to their fathers for guidance in the process of differentiating between the desire of belonging to a group and drawing limits on group behavior. The character named Atticus Finch in Harper Lee's classic novel *To Kill a Mockingbird* is an excellent example of such a father. In a Southern town drenched in race prejudice and imbued with Jim Crow values, Finch stands up for what he believes to be right, and his latency-age children, knowing full well what is not right, learn to stand up with him against the community's pressure.

The importance of a mentoring father figure during this period is essential to a son's healthy development. In a father's absence, many boys are left to negotiate latency on their own, which may leave them deficient in regulating work-related self-esteem; and then, in turn, they may experience "father hunger" for a validating masculine presence for the remainder of childhood, and most likely their entire lives. Regardless of the boy's areas of interest or talents, a mentoring father can recognize and help his son to develop his skills, while providing sufficient realistic feedback so that the boy can pursue his ambitions and publicly express his talents.

Carlos, an eighteen-year-old whom I had seen in therapy for a number of years, was one such young man in need of a father's mentoring presence, particularly during his latency years. His own distant yet highly critical father had left the family when Carlos was only seven, a time when he was very much in need of mentoring in terms of his talents, skills, and ambitions. Lacking a father to encourage him to develop his sense of industry, Carlos eventually sought solace in music, for which he showed great aptitude. Despite his love of both composing and performing, he was very reluctant to play for others; only after a school music instructor encouraged him did he perform at the junior high school talent show. Nonetheless, he remained terrified of being criticized, fearful that his music was "trivial and didn't amount to much."

Despite these fears, Carlos had composed many rock songs by the time I met him, and had performed at the community college he attended to much acclaim. During one of our sessions, he excitedly told me, with a huge and disbelieving smile: "I had three encores! It's like they can't get enough of me." However, when I asked him if he might share his songs with me, he refused. He didn't want me to hear them. Though—or perhaps because—he trusted and depended so heavily on me, more than anyone else in his life, he was afraid that I'd find his music superficial and his lyrics sappy, much as he assumed that his disinterested and disparaging father would. He felt certain that something valuable in our relationship would be permanently destroyed were he to expose this side of himself to me.

As Carlos and I discussed his fears and feelings over the course of many sessions, we were able to understand how his refusal to play his songs for me amounted to a preemptive strike: If I did hear his music, I could possibly be disappointed in him, which would be a devastating consequence for a father-hungry young man. His cynicism, which he projected onto me, served to protect him from being let down or betrayed. It took four months of talking until Carlos felt comfortable and secure enough to play a newly recorded CD of his music for me, and together we celebrated his creativity as well as his psychological breakthrough.

The profound need for active paternal mentoring in groups is illustrated brilliantly in William Golding's novel *Lord of the Flies* (1962). The story involves a group of unmentored, latency-age and early adolescent boys shipwrecked on an island where absolute freedom and the absence of limits and laws soon lead to a chaotic nightmare. The hunger for the fathering dimension is indicated by the founding of a pagan cult worshiping a pig's head. Murder follows, and order and salvation are restored only at the very end of the novel when a British officer, symbolizing the absent masculine influence, arrives.

TEACHING A SENSE OF INDUSTRY

Boys between six and twelve years old focus on both industry and competence as they come to appreciate the ethos of productivity. They like to feel useful and busy, to make things, and to share in both the planning and construction. Through goal-directed activity, they seek to gain admission to the very alluring world of adult men. Along the way, they discover the pleasure that accompanies productive activity. Latency-age boys are riveted by how things work. The idea of being useful comes into sharper focus. During this time, fathers show their care by actively collaborating with their sons in doing productive activities, imparting what the child and adolescent psychiatrist James Herzog calls the "how do you do it" mode.[5] Preferably, a father is able to do things that his son appreciates, and in turn, is experienced as skilled and capable. As a result, his son will internalize a notion of masculinity that is associated strongly with doing rather than simply understanding or thinking about doing. "Just Do It!" as the Nike motto proclaims, exemplifies this spirit of middle childhood.

Boys of this age need to feel a sense of competence and pride, and their fathers' opinions and admiration carry tremendous weight. Consequently, latency-age boys are exceptionally attuned to their fathers' reactions to their productive behavior. Although fathers remain their most sought-after teachers, they also seek out teachers, parents of other children, and men who represent occupations that are visible, comprehensible, and accessible, such as firemen, policemen, or construction workers.

Teaching mastery of tasks, however, is not always easy. Many boys get angry when their fathers try to instruct them. A father, in turn, may back off, not wanting to engage in the ongoing battle of convincing his son that he has much to learn. But when a father doesn't give up, when he hangs in and mildly but firmly encourages his son to rise to the challenge of learning new things, the boy will discover that he can accomplish things he never would have imagined on his own, nor would he have been able to achieve by means of fantasy and play alone. Such accomplishments then are

the product of practicality and logic, and as a result, the boy carries with him a feeling of competence and what the renowned psychoanalyst Erik Erikson termed the "sense of industry."[6]

Similarly—and equally important—fathers give their sons permission to struggle with hard tasks and, in certain cases, to fail
to be successful. Boys learn this as they watch how their fathers
respond to their own shortcomings, failures, and limitations.
Seeing and acknowledging that their father is imperfect is much
more important than thinking of him as an expert in every
endeavor. In fact, a boy learns to internalize his father's reactions
to his own mistakes and frustration as an emotional template for
dealing with struggles, vulnerabilities, and limitations of his own.

An example from my own experience is quite illustrative.
Alex, my eight-year-old son, was watching me coach his older sister, Maya's, basketball game. Near the end of the game I became
very frustrated when the referee made a blatant mistake, and I
overreacted, incurring a technical foul that cost our team the
game. As I drove the kids home, we commiserated about the
injustice of the call and laughed about my foolish reaction that
compounded the situation. I acknowledged my errant behavior
and our talking together about it brought us closer, particularly
since it revealed my own limitations in a realm where I had until
then appeared to be so proficient. Alex spoke about this incident
for years and loved to have me recount the story of how I yelled
at the referee. He chides me even to this day, with more than a
touch of irony and delight, whenever I give vent to some of my
more unruly feelings as he playfully asks, "Hey, Dad, aren't you
supposed to be a psychologist?"

The father who can admit and show his own limitations and
mistakes to his son while simultaneously supporting the boy in
his failings teaches his son how to feel confident and proud
despite obstacles and setbacks. In this fashion, the father is giv-

ing his son permission to be a fallible human being who can express emotional vulnerability and expose himself to physical and cognitive challenges. In the course of looking up to his admired father, the son is able to identify as well with his father's human shortcomings and gradually form a more realistic ideal for himself. Such a boy can more easily give up his grandiose demands for self-perfection, thereby becoming more self-accepting. He won't feel the need to become a cardboard Superman for whom any one mistake may prove fatal.[7]

A son's healthy sense of his father's vulnerabilities (and strengths) is poignantly expressed in the writings of a seven-year-old boy entitled "A tiny poem to my Dad":

> *You are like a strong kite*
> *waiting for the wind*
> *and the sweet snow that loves me*
> *and the hurt tiger that needs my help.*[8]

Fathers who cannot admit to their shortcomings transmit the message that men shouldn't have these frailties or limits, let alone expose them. As a result, their sons are implicitly encouraged to maintain an illusionary sense of omnipotence—an unrealistic notion of manliness. This is commonly manifest when a boy starts believing that he shouldn't try to pursue interests and activities at which he's not particularly adept, an outlook that proves very constraining and counterproductive. Unfortunately, many boys and later, men, are restrained by the feeling that it's only permissible to do what they are already good at.

How fathers teach is as important as *what* they teach. The more attuned a father is to his son's needs, the better he will be able to tailor the lesson to the student. He'll know how much material the boy can absorb at one sitting, whether to appeal to his son's intellectual, visual, or kinesthetic pathway, and at what point his son will begin tuning him out. He will also better know how to alternate work and play, how to encourage unique talents, and how to recognize outstanding effort. With this information, he can help his son's other teachers or mentors—the boy's mother, schoolteacher, and soccer coach or music tutor—by suggesting how they might best guide and teach his boy.

A patient of mine named Fred recently described the nature of this sometimes difficult process. Fred, a manager at an appliance store, related how his ten-year-old son Jimmy kept calling him into the den to set up the DVD player for him. Finally, Fred said, "Hey, I've got a great idea. Let's go through the directions together, so next time you can do it yourself." Jimmy declined and instead asked his father to just set it up for him.

But Fred refused, telling Jimmy he wanted him to learn how to do it for himself. Jimmy protested once more. Although he knew that it would be easier and quicker to just do what Jimmy asked, at least in the short run, Fred nonetheless held his ground. He added, "When you learn how to do it yourself, you can watch a DVD whenever you want."

"No, Dad, you just do it," Jimmy whined. Fred, tired after a long day's work, felt himself losing patience with his son, and wanted nothing more than to give in to Jimmy so he could sit down with the newspaper. But, Fred proudly told me, he managed to maintain his position of authority despite his son's escalating opposition, and his resolve paid off. Jimmy eventually acquiesced, though his attitude was less than pleasant throughout the learning session with his dad. Within a few weeks, however, Jimmy became adept at using both the DVD and the entire home entertainment system. And Fred said that he could detect a proud smile on Jimmy's face whenever the boy used the system.

· · ·

The idea of father as master teacher and son as apprentice is as old as the world's earliest myths. Rumi, the thirteenth-century Sufi mystic poet, articulated this pressing need boys have to receive specific guidance directed toward mastery from their fathers:

> *Think that you're gliding out from the face of a*
> *cliff like an eagle.*
> *Think you're walking like a tiger walks by him-*
> *self in the forest.*
> *You're most handsome when you're after food.*
> *Spend less time with nightingales and peacocks.*
> *One is just a voice, the other just a color.*[9]

HELPING SONS REGULATE THEIR EMOTIONS

For boys to achieve mastery over certain skills, they need to learn to regulate their often intense emotions. Otherwise, unchecked feelings turn into static, which can easily undermine the quest for competence. In this sense, fathers help their sons to pay attention to their feelings as opposed to ignoring or suppressing them. Then the boys begin to sublimate their emotions in the service of achieving a desired goal.

One way that fathers accomplish this is by helping their sons learn to shift gears from one level of emotional arousal to another. During this period when fathers and sons roughhouse, the son doesn't simply learn to relish male physicality as he did when he was younger. In a much more complex interaction, the son reads the father for cues at the same time that the father reads the son. That is, an attuned dad will know that his son is paying close attention to how he behaves in order to learn how to behave himself, and so the father will modulate his responses to his son, applying more force and easing up as needed. Because of the quality of this paternal attention, roughhousing turns into a real-life laboratory in which boys study how much force is too much, how to judge when someone is playacting or exhibiting genuine emotion, and how to take on a more powerful opponent without losing heart. In time, the boy will generalize what he's learned about reading his father's cues to read the cues of others.

In addition then to deliberate, intentional instruction, boys also learn by observing their fathers, frequently during tradition-ally shared activities and play. In so doing, fathers serve as mod-els, showing their sons how men thoughtfully and appropriately deal with difficult emotions and situations. Another way fathers help their sons to harness their emotions is by modeling what the psychologist Carol Gilligan refers to as a "male mode of moral-ity," which specifically emphasizes more abstract conceptions of rules, fairness, and justice rather than the more concrete notions of relationship and connection.[10]

For example, I was told a story once about a seven-year-old boy named Chad who got in trouble at school when he forgot to bring in a note saying that his friend could come home with him; without this note, the friend could not visit. By the time Chad got home, he was very upset, disappointed that his friend couldn't play, and fearful that he would be angry with him for ruining their afternoon. When his mother spoke to him about this, she asked him to think about the fact that he let his friend down and may have even hurt his feelings. In taking this approach, she was trying to focus Chad's thoughts on emotional and relationship issues which, according to Gilligan, form the basis of women's morality. Chad's father, however, focused on how important a commitment is; his son had promised to get a signed note from his parents so his friend could come home with him, and he had failed to follow through. He spoke to his son about how he needed to "play by the rules," to respect the ideals of fair play and justice, and learn to operate within certain frameworks.

Needless to say, a father's control over his son's burgeoning curiosities and impulses toward action is far from complete, as the Greek myth of Daedalus and Icarus reminds us. Daedalus was an inventor and master craftsman who designed the complex maze known as the Labyrinth in which he and his son Icarus were eventually imprisoned.

In order to escape, Daedalus provided Icarus with wings of wax and feathers, and painstakingly instructed him on how to fly. But "Fly too near the sun," he cautioned the youth, "and the sun will melt the wax and you'll fall into the sea. Fly too near the water," he continued, "and the feathers will become damp and heavy, and will fail as well."

At first, Icarus heeded his father's advice. But after a short time, intoxicated by the thrill of flying, he soared into the sky. Just as his father had predicted, the wax melted and the youth plunged into the sea. Daedalus, like countless fathers before and since, tried to instruct his son to the best of his ability, only to have the son reject his father's lesson, this time with disastrous results. Acknowledging the limits of our ability to teach our sons is one of fatherhood's most bitter lessons.

ENCOURAGING ABSTRACT THINKING

To explore the more intricate ways in which a father has an impact on his son's cognitive development, we need to think of the older man archetypically as "the Father." According to the psychoanalysts Carl Jung and Jacques Lacan, among others, the Father principle represents order.[11] This is an age-old theme in Western civilization. Consider Zeus and Thor of Greek and Norse mythology, respectively; they were both "sky fathers," who ruled over a pantheon of other gods as well as over mortals. The opening verse of the Gospel According to St. John ("In the beginning was the Word, and the Word was with God, and the Word was God") can be interpreted to mean that the word, and the type of ordering intelligence it represents, is considered the first product of God the Father when He created the world.

Why is language given so much power? In essence, language, formulated into laws, imposes order and makes distinctions from the undifferentiated swirl of primal, unconscious impulse, feeling, and thought. The father, as he has traditionally been understood, not only possesses words but also the authority that words bestow. Lacan maintains that what he terms the "Law of the Father" introduces the child to the world of symbolic thought by disrupting the child's symbiotic bond to his mother. That is, after the mother introduces her son to, and thereby becomes associated with, the world of feeling, it's then the father's role to furnish his son with language he can use to understand and express what he is feeling, as well as to usher him into the realm of higher-level mental functioning. In short, words and language help the little boy to develop an awareness of time and, consequently, individuate from the gratifying world associated with his mother.

According to this way of thinking, the unique temperaments and specific characteristics of the mother and the father in any family are not always the most significant determinants of what their son looks for from them or how he relates to each of them. It rarely matters that in given situations the mother is more rationally minded and "intellectual" while the father may be impulsive and highly sensitive; because of what mothers and fathers represent in our culture, a son will still look to his father to bring order to his world, particularly a son who is latency-aged. This is also due to the fact that no matter how intellectually competent his mother might be, this boy's ties to her are primal and biological. As he attempts to move away from her, he experiences conflict and looks to his father for help, who by nature of being different from the mother offers a fundamentally different way of looking at the world.

Fathers who are unable to use their paternal authority to help their sons learn to use words in order to regulate their impulses and emotions make it difficult for their sons to leave the emotional orbit of their mothers and venture off into the world that requires navigating among intense conflict and difficult feelings. When fathers resort to violent action and physical abuse to express difficult feelings in lieu of affect-regulating words, the detrimental effects will impact their sons in profound ways throughout their lives. In particular, the abusive father not only fails to protect and guide his son toward using language as a tool for self-regulation, but causes the boy to try unconsciously to structure his life in specific ways in order to deal with what inevitably is becoming internalized from his "abusive" father.

Of course, many men who've been physically and emotionally abused remain unconsciously identified with their violent fathers. Though they often carry considerable guilt and psychic pain about it, they keep the so-called "cycle of abuse" alive in their current relationships with partners and children. Other men try hard *not* to be anything like their violent fathers, disavowing any similarities while attempting to behave in opposite fashion. However, it is not so easy to transform what remains psychically active though commonly hidden from conscious awareness; thus, these men frequently become overly self-critical and depressed. The legacy of abuse is difficult to break. It requires that a man look deep inside himself, often with skilled professional help, in order to consciously face the internal consequences of his father's behavior.

A boy whose father is unable to use words constructively to absorb and contain difficult feelings, but instead expresses his feelings in violent action, often grows up fearing not only his father but also his own aggression. This may render him overly dependent on his mother, and subsequently on other women who seem to represent safety from the uncontrollable danger associated with men. For example, I worked with Peter, a boyishly handsome, divorced father in his early forties. Though a successful artist, he was lonely and depressed, experiencing himself as "a little boy lost." He dreaded conflict and had a hard time asserting himself. Women were drawn to his gentle sweetness, only to become fed up with his passivity and lack of commitment. Hungry for male friends, he was also troubled by his inability to be a strong fatherly influence on his nine-year-old son.

During our first meetings, Peter revealed that he felt terrorized by his violent father, who divorced his mother when he was eight. In subsequent sessions, however, he focused on his agonizingly unsuccessful efforts to establish boundaries with his weak yet invasive mother. One day, he tearfully recounted an incident shortly before his parents divorced when his father fired a gun in the house during an argument with Peter's uncle. Although no one was hurt, Peter shook as he relived hearing gunshots and recalled seeing bullet holes in the ceiling. He told me that he had never recovered from that afternoon, that he remained "haunted by those gunshots and my father's rage." He reported several incidents in which his drunken father terrorized him physically, particularly when Peter dared to disagree with him. He then looked at me and said sadly, "I need to get angry, to feel angry with you, and lots of other people in my life, but I can't, and I'm afraid I never will." Peter wished for a strong yet restrained father, who could use words to help tolerate forceful emotion, conflict, and ambivalence without becoming abusive. Because his father hadn't been able to provide this for him, he grew up fearful of any negative feelings and was deficient in his capacity to talk about strong feeling. Peter's own aggression particularly terrified him because it seemed uncontainable, promising only destruction and abandonment.

As our work together progressed and Peter could begin to safely experience reliving the way he felt with his own father, he couldn't escape from his distress about having angry feelings toward me. When I urged Peter to explore these feelings, he explained: "I am afraid of being dissatisfied with you because if I am, I'll get angry and there'll be nothing left but rage. That's all I'll be, an empty shell filled with rage."

I realized that he was also afraid that if he were to get angry with me, I'd lose control and retaliate, effectively abandoning him as his own father did. What Peter needed was a father figure who could modulate both his own and his son's feelings through language; in other words, an analyst who could face his aggression and anger head-on, so that Peter could tolerate such feelings in himself and ultimately learn ways to express them through language that wouldn't be so destructive. Fortunately, over the course of a long and successful analysis, Peter learned that he (and I) could contain and integrate his own "darker," more negative and aggressive impulses through their direct expression in words. As a result, he became able to set appropriate boundaries in a challenging yet calm way for his now teenaged son. This was no small accomplishment for Peter, whose own father hadn't been able to model emotional regulation.

As this case suggests, one of the most important ways that fathers teach their sons to regulate their emotions is to modulate feelings through language and subsequently by imparting certain concepts. The Swiss developmental psychologist Jean Piaget labeled this period in a child's life the stage of "concrete operations," referring to the ways in which children begin to leave the world of imagination and fantasy for the world of logic and reality.[12] When they were younger, they felt the need to act immediately on every urge; now, they use language and concepts to modulate and temper these urges. This helps them to maintain their psychic equilibrium.

I once observed a ten-year-old boy, Lonny, the catcher of his Little League baseball team, who refused to leave the dugout after losing a closely contested game. He had been guarding the plate when the other team's player scored the winning run, though Lonny insisted that this player was in fact out, not safe, which would have given his team another chance to bat. Everyone had left the playing field except for Lonny, who sat sulking in his uniform.

I was particularly struck by the skill his father used as he waited for a while and then walked over to Lonny, telling him, "It's hard losing a close game like that. You feel angry, and I understand, but it's not okay to act out your anger in front of everyone, especially the team that beat you. They won and deserve respect. You can get angry at home, but now you have to collect yourself. That's what sportsmanship is all about." Lonny didn't respond at first, but after a few minutes, the word "sportsmanship" seemed to register with him. As a result of this exchange with his father, Lonny now has a word to cling to and a quality toward which to strive. The word also tells him what behaviors are appropriate when and under what circumstances it's acceptable to express certain intense emotions.

This marks the beginning of a boy's learning to regulate his emotions through understanding the power of words. In chapter 3, Claude was able to help his son, Roger, realize, through use of language, that his mother didn't hate him after he spilled his milk but was merely angry. Similarly, Lonny's father was also able to show his son that he doesn't have to rely solely on emotions or reflexes when confronted with disappointment and feelings of loss; rather, he has a very wide range of ways to respond to such situations.

A father's impact on his son's cognitive development lasts a lifetime. Cal, a patient of mine, recently spoke of his father who died when he was fifteen. Although Cal was still angry with and disappointed in his self-absorbed father, who had abandoned the family when Cal was about nine, he realized that the man had given him an important gift: the ability to think. "I didn't see him much after the divorce," Cal recalled, "but whenever I did, we'd end up talking about how things work, how you can't just accept everything as it appears but must analyze things more deeply, and how important it is to question authority. He taught me to think critically, and thankfully, I do so every day." For this, he added, he'd always be grateful.

THE FATHER'S RECIPROCAL LEARNING

But the learning is not just one-way. Fathers often have something to learn about mastery, emotional regulation, and playfulness from their latency-aged sons. Moreover, by actively helping their sons to master the physical, emotional, and cognitive tasks of middle childhood, fathers vicariously satisfy their own needs to continue to develop and achieve mastery. Through their mutual and active engagement, father and son each benefit; it is not uncommon to discover that a son "teaches" his father an important lesson along the way.

For instance, George, a man who consulted me for help, would sit devotedly in the bleachers week after week to watch his eleven-year-old son Ivan play soccer. Ivan was an outstanding clarinet player and an exceptional student, but his athletic prowess was negligible. Yet, even though he rarely spent more than a couple of minutes on the field, he always played his heart out, and eventually his teammates began to appreciate his devotion and his superb sense of humor.

During one particularly rough game, when Ivan committed two costly fouls, George had a hard time keeping his seat, particularly as he watched the other fathers basking in their sons' successes. He wanted nothing more than to get up and leave; but he knew how much Ivan was counting on him to stay.

Even though Ivan's final blunder had cost his team the game, George told him that he was proud of the way he kept his head up and could enjoy playing despite his struggles, before adding, "Since it takes courage for a man to face his mistakes and limitations and still pursue what's important for him."

A few days later, George blew a deadline assignment at the architectural firm where he worked—the project he'd been working on just wasn't ready. He felt miserable. But during a sleepless night, he found his mind returning to Ivan's most recent soccer game and how, despite his embarrassment, his son had hung in. George was filled with respect for his son and recalled what he had told Ivan about facing his "mistakes and limitations." George then realized that he had learned something from watching his eleven-year-old boy. "You know," he thought before falling back to sleep, "I've got my own limitations and I screwed up badly, but hell, I know what I want to accomplish at work and tomorrow I can get back on track."

. . .

Fathers who shepherd their sons into the world of team sports or physical activity often end up rediscovering their own playful sides, the lighthearted selves they had to put aside while they struggled to get through school, find jobs, and establish relationships with their partners. Just by hanging out with their sons, men—particularly those who are more socially isolated, or on a fast-paced achievement track—often find that their playful, more freely competitive "boyish" selves reawaken. Many engaged fathers reacquaint themselves with the boy inside who played ball until it was too dark to see; staged marathon poker tournaments; stayed up all night to talk about girls, cars, and sports; and later argued about the meaning of life while sharing some beers.

For those boys whose fathers can act as mentors, for those fathers as well, latency is often a halcyon time when father and son discover the pleasures of friendship, male camaraderie, and reciprocal approval. Sadly, some of these pleasures may prove transient. With each passing day, latency-age boys approach adolescence, a time when the father-son bond will be challenged in ways that neither father nor son, working side by side in their basement carpentry shop or tossing a ball back and forth in the backyard, could anticipate.

6

FROM HERO TO FALLEN HERO

*Don't ever tell anybody anything. If you do,
you start missing everybody.*

—J. D. SALINGER, *The Catcher in the Rye*[1]

Outrageous, conformist, turbulent, despairing, desperate, crazy, ecstatic—these words only begin to describe the breathtaking roller coaster of the emotionally intense, hormone-fueled teenage years. Teenagers' shifting moods are hard to predict, let alone tolerate, fluctuating wildly from grandiose self-love to self-hatred and despair; from love to hate, often directed at the same person; from passionate crushes to cool indifference; from over-involvement to icy detachment and withdrawal. Very rapidly, adolescents have to come to terms with their changing bodies, outrageous urges, and radically altering minds. Boys are, more-over, faced with three essential tasks: to begin to formulate their own identities while incorporating all the changes they're undergoing; to separate from their families, particularly from their fathers; and to begin to come to terms with their feelings of loss.

The father-son bond unavoidably changes radically during adolescence. Until now, if a father has been available and is good enough, he and his son most likely enjoy a rather steady, congen-ial relationship, a continuation of their childhood ties. But dur-ing a boy's adolescence, his feelings about his father become more volatile and unpredictable. Young teenage boys look up to their fathers, often idealize them, as they search for models to guide them through their identity confusion. Whether they admit it or not, they believe their dad is the strongest, the most ath-letic, the handiest, the funniest, the best driver, the smartest, and so on and so on.

The challenge for fathers and sons at this stage of development is to accept the idealization without taking it too much to heart, because soon enough, idealization turns into its opposite. By middle adolescence, boys often become much more critical of their fathers, paving the way for yet another change in late ado-lescence, when boys tend to not only distance themselves from their dads but devalue parental authority.

It's a difficult time for fathers, many of whom are confronting the discontents, worries, and surprises common to middle age. As they begin to accept the fact that they have lost their "young" boys, as well as youthful versions of themselves, they contend with loss, impotence, resignation, and their own mortality. At the same time, many experience vivid memories of their relationship with their own fathers as they struggle to handle a myriad of emotions with their sons. Though they may fight and frequently seem at odds, fathers and their teenage sons are in fact struggling with identical issues of identity, differentiation, and loss.

SONS REVISITING IDENTITY ISSUES

"Who am I?" This is the crucial question that plagues teenage boys. During adolescence, boys need to form an identity that's relatively stable and secure as well as flexible. It is not that the self is born in adolescence—that happens during infancy—but rather that teenagers seek a sense of identity as the boundaries of the "me" and the "not-me" become more clearly established. Because all future growth depends on how well teenagers negotiate this quest to define themselves, a father's empathy, acceptance, and support, in combination with appropriate limit setting, are critical.

For a teenage boy, trying to secure an identity is like finding firm footing in a boat buffeted by twenty-foot waves. It's not uncommon for teens to feel as if they go to sleep with one body and wake up with another; the new one having more hair, larger genitals, and a voice that cracks when they begin a sentence. At the same time, surging hormones unleash familiar and often alarming bodily and sexual impulses.

Boys are especially needy of understanding fathers to negotiate these physical changes. Girls, in one respect, usually have an easier time of it, as most mothers are aware of their role to prepare their daughters for the onset of menstruation. Unfortunately, there is often no such instruction passing from father to son. As a result, many boys find themselves surprised, confused, and frequently ashamed of their first bodily experiences, such as nocturnal emissions, of which they may have received no warning from parental figures.

Masturbatory impulses also intensify in teenage boys; it's a way for them to try on their sexuality in their newly maturing bodies. As a result, they harbor feelings of confusion, excitement, and shame about boundary and privacy issues. In many families, boys find themselves arguing more directly with their mothers than with their fathers. As part of their sexual awakening, boys may find themselves having incestuous thoughts about their mothers, which are experienced as so disturbing that a boy needs to renounce not only his pull toward his mom but *any* feeling of closeness he has toward her. Manifest feelings of repulsion and aversion toward any sign of a mother's sexuality are often expressed in the rudest of ways in order to mask the teenage boy's more unconscious erotic interest. These unacceptable feelings are repressed; instead, the teenage boy proclaims his affection for girls who ostensibly appear nothing like his mother.

These rapid-fire physical changes challenge the boy's sense of his masculinity and gender role identity as well as his previous position regarding choice of love object: does he like boys or girls? It may seem very confusing, especially since this is a time when fantasies derived from repressed oedipal, incestuous wishes for his mother may resurface, as well as forbidden feelings toward a sister, which can both interfere with and spur on his desire for girls. On the other hand, as much as he hungers for male companionship and may even want to experiment sexually with other boys, he dreads being labeled as homosexual. Homophobia often haunts boys at this age, and some feel the need to rigidly defend their more fragile adolescent sense of masculinity.

Fathers can encourage their sons to accept and integrate their tender and loving feelings toward other males. They accomplish this by maintaining safe, non-threatening, affectionate relationships with their sons (in the best cases, this continues what has been established long ago). By reassuring their sons that all men worry occasionally about their manliness and their feelings toward other men, fathers adeptly model how loving relationships can enrich rather than threaten one's sense of masculinity in the course of supporting their son's closeness with other males. This is most likely accomplished when a father can continue to openly express his affection toward his son while simultaneously appreciating his son's phase-specific concerns about being viewed as "gay." Teenage boys are searching for ways to express their warm feelings toward close friends, favorite teachers, and other males, and they observe and listen closely to what their fathers say and do in this realm, regardless of how disinterested they may seem.

Some boys, however, particularly at this stage, discover that they do have strong homosexual feelings and erotic urges, and perhaps are gay. This may prove difficult for many fathers to accept. Yet these boys have the same strong need for their fathers to be affectionate, understanding, and to support their budding sense of masculinity as do heterosexual boys. If fathers withdraw, criticize, reject, or act ashamed of their sons, the boys will have greater difficulty accepting themselves, particularly in relation to their sexuality. The stronger the relationship between a gay son and father at this point, the more likely the relationship will endure through the rest of adolescence and into adulthood. In fact, those fathers who are able to embrace their gay sons often find that they achieve a more nuanced and profound understanding of what it really means to be a man.

David, for example, the father of fourteen-year-old Jeremy, came to see me some years ago after finding a gay pornography site on his son's computer. Distraught, David went on to explain that he'd also learned that his son was involved in a relationship with an older boy. Although he loved his son, he was tormented by the fact that Jeremy was in all likelihood gay.

"What does it mean to you that Jeremy might be gay?" I asked him. That question enabled us to explore David's fears about homosexuality and the revulsion he felt. He also talked about his profound sense of sadness—ever since Jeremy's birth, David had fantasized that his son would marry a girl like his mother and have children of his own; that father and son would stay close, finding ways to escape for their annual summer camping trip. Over time, as David felt free to voice his fantasies and face his real sense of regret, he began to accept that Jeremy was a gay young man. Though they had many rocky times, father and son eventually came together again, bonding over their similarities and differences. By the time Jeremy graduated from high school, there was no prouder father in the audience than David, especially when Jeremy was cited by the student council and given a rousing ovation by his classmates for founding the school's Gay Students Alliance.

SONS EVOKING FATHERS' IDENTITY ISSUES

Fathers of teenage boys grapple with their own identities as well as with their sons'. Adolescence and middle age often coincide, and many men reflect on questions they may not have considered since they were teenagers themselves: "Who am I, especially now that my son is turning into a young man? What happened to the young woman I married? What do I want to make of my life? What changes do I want to make while I still can?"

Many men don't want to confront this turning point in their lives until their sons force the issue. When Joe first came to see me, he was extremely upset that his sixteen-year-old son Adam was "rejecting" him at every turn. They'd always been so close, Joe explained, but now Adam had a girlfriend and a life at school that Joe knew nothing about. Whenever Joe tried to talk to his son, Adam would snap at him and say that everything was fine, "and anyway, it's private, so stop asking!" And then he'd slam his bedroom door shut.

"You're a spoiled brat," Joe told his son after one of these particular episodes. "I'm your father, and I'm entitled to know about you!"

"You're a nosey little man who can't get along without his wife and children," Adam shouted through the door. "You can't do anything for yourself—your whole life is organized around me. It's about time you got some friends and a life of your own!"

Adam was closing the door on his father both figuratively and literally so that he could craft an identity distinct and apart from that within the family. But Joe could only think about his own loss. "I've given him so much, and now he wants nothing to do with me, that ungrateful kid," Joe told me. His grief was palpable, though he was experiencing it, as many men do, as anger directed toward his son.

As Joe and I discussed the situation, it became clearer to him that what Adam had said was essentially true. Most teenagers have a laserlike "bullshit detector"—an uncanny ability to sniff out the very truths their parents are trying to ignore. "I don't have any friends besides my wife, and my life has been totally wrapped up in working and in raising Adam and his older sister, Joelle," Joe painfully admitted, before adding, "I don't know who I am these days except some kind of working guy and a 'good dad'—or at least I thought I was."

Joe's realization, sparked by his son's honest observation, signaled a breakthrough in our work together. Joe was able to recognize that just as Adam was establishing his identity as a young man, he too was undergoing his own "identity crisis" as a middle-aged man confronting an aging self, one in need of a new identity of its own. Being a "good dad" would no longer serve as the core of his identity, as his son was too old for that now. He'd have to forge a new one, however painfully.

Within several months, Joe began to renew an old interest in photography, spending Sunday afternoons walking through his neighborhood taking photos. After Adam went off to college, the two were still at odds, but Joe consoled himself by spending hours in the darkroom. When I last heard from Joe soon after Adam's law school graduation, I was pleased to learn that the two had revived a respectful and close adult relationship.

This case exemplifies how a son's derisive behavior can push his father to take stock of himself by facing his own midlife identity issues. This crucial challenge of middle adulthood commonly occurs later when the child actually leaves home, and lies beneath the so-called "empty nest syndrome." As we'll see in the next chapter, the need to find a new identity that is less tied to being a parent tends to occur later for fathers than it does for mothers.

THE "SECOND INDIVIDUATION" FROM THE FATHER

Over the course of adolescence, the "psychological navel cord" first frays, then weakens, and finally gets severed, as teenagers assert their right and need to exist separately from their parents. The adolescent psychoanalyst Peter Blos calls this "the second individuation."[2] The first time, when the boy was a toddler, he removed himself from his mother's world in order to embrace his father's. Mothers bore the brunt of this early separation. However, when the teenage boy is leaving his parents behind to form his own relationship to the world, it's often the father who is the primary target.

This phase can be particularly difficult for fathers who had until recently often been put on a pedestal. While being so admired, fathers find it relatively easy to indirectly support their adolescent sons' new identities, primarily by interceding with their wife during a son's arguments with her. As he intuits his son's needs, the father translates his teenager's inchoate wishes and assures him (and the boy's mother) that he is developing normally. In this fashion, he may once again seem like the "rescuer" who helps his teenage boy differentiate from his close tie to his mother. But as adolescence progresses, boys increasingly come to see their bonds to their fathers as childish and experience these attachments as regressive, pulling them back into boyhood. In a complete reversal, they may disengage from and ultimately deidealize their fathers, often viewing them as disappointing, inadequate, limited, unfair, old, clumsy, hypocritical, and overly rigid. A hero no longer, the father has fallen: he's no longer *the* authority that he once was.

A colleague of mine recalled to me how he'd always looked up to his father as tall and strong, strict but fair, and fun-loving. Yet the two had a mighty clash the summer of 1969 when my friend turned sixteen years old and wanted to drive with friends to Woodstock, the epic musical festival. "My father heard me talking on the phone making arrangements," my friend explained. "When he came into my room wearing his pajamas, I was so startled to see him; he looked shrunken. He began explaining why I couldn't go, that he feared for my safety. I got up from my chair, walked over to him—it seemed as if I towered over him—and said, 'The things you're concerned about are ridiculous. I'm going and you can't do anything to stop me.' He looked me in the eye, and we both knew that I was right, he couldn't stop me. And in that moment I felt nothing but disgust for him, for his smallness, his weakness, his powerlessness." My colleague recalled sadly how he and his father didn't have another meaningful conversation again for several years.

Why do older teenage boys need to devalue their fathers? Deeply engrossed in determining their identity, adolescents constantly reevaluate their own self-image in terms of how well liked or how good-looking, smart, or talented they are. Exquisitely attuned to their own inadequacies, they can't help but notice the shortcomings in their fathers as well. How much easier it is—and in many respects how much healthier—for a boy to displace his anger toward a father who is increasingly seen as less than ideal, rather than to direct his disappointment toward his own confused and still quite fragile sense of self.

In turning away from their fathers, it's almost as if some teens are bent on obliterating their need for them. Many adolescents—particularly those who had been close to their fathers, or whose fathers are clinging and needy—may wish to kill the older man, however unacceptable and unconscious this feeling remains. Moreover, in asserting their right to a separate existence from their father, most teenage boys unconsciously feel as if they are killing him. The adolescent boy experiences growing up as a form of homicide, tantamount to the "murder of his parents."[3]

For example, Donald, a seventeen-year-old former patient of mine, initially came to therapy because he was getting behind in school and was terribly anxious most of the time. As we talked, it became clearer he was terrified of his fifty-one-year-old physician father dying suddenly, although he was in excellent health. Donald often dreamt about his father dying. In one dream, Donald was at the wheel, his father in the passenger seat beside him, when they collided head-on with another car. Donald was fine, but his father was badly hurt. Yet Donald felt immobilized, as he often did in these dreams, unable even to pick up the fallen cell phone on the road beside him to call for assistance as he helplessly watched his father stop breathing. Not surprisingly, he awoke feeling terribly disturbed.

Over time, though, we were gradually able to understand Donald's ambivalent wishes to become more independent of his strong and dominant father, and his accompanying fears about doing so. Donald was afraid that he would let his dad down, that he wouldn't follow in his father's footsteps and become a successful professional. Eventually, he was able to face another truth: that he hated the fact that his father's opinion of him mattered so much to him. As Donald explored his entwined wishes—both to be free of his father and to admit candidly how much he hated as well as loved his father—his anxiety began to abate and his schoolwork to improve. Not overnight, but in time, Donald became increasingly comfortable with his teenage need to find his own path in life. Yet his dream remains a testament to the very natural yet unconscious fear and wish that by killing one's father, one begins to become an independent man.

The process of disillusionment and disengagement is often quite painful as it leaves boys feeling empty, lost, alienated, and hungry for someone who can compensate for the loss of their father and offer support. They naturally seek out the company of peers or other male adults, such as uncles, coaches, and teachers, as substitute fathers. Some will resort to idealizing men who may be radically different from their fathers, such as goth or hip-hop stars, religious celibates, or political leaders who challenge their father's values. However, when the teenage boy's relationship with his father is more problematic, he will seek most all of his guidance elsewhere, oftentimes from risky outside sources as he becomes highly dependent on peer culture.[4]

For their part, fathers need to find ways of dealing with this distancing in a manner that supports rather than undermines the son's need to separate. I once accompanied my friend Paul to his son's soccer game. As fifteen-year-old Mark warmed up with his team, Paul stood on the sidelines recollecting when he coached Mark's first soccer team, recalling how they'd practice together weekends and evenings. As time passed, however, Mark stopped wanting to practice with his dad. "It's because of me that he loves sports—he even gets his athletic ability from me—but these days, all I'm good for is to drive him to his games," Paul said bitterly.

Suddenly, there were cheers from the field as Mark scored a goal. Paul put aside his painful thoughts to applaud his son, smiling and giving his son a thumbs-up, while Mark merely nodded and ran to his teammates and coach to accept their joyful embraces. Years ago, Paul would have erupted in wild celebration, though he knew now that if he were to display such emotions, Mark would be mortified. However, by containing his own feelings and considering the needs of his son at this moment rather than his own—allowing Mark to celebrate his goal with his friends instead of with him—Paul enabled Mark to think of himself as a competent individual, separate from his own family, who would increasingly seek support, relief, and stimulation from outside the family rather than within.

As their teenage sons struggle with independence, middle-aged fathers are engaged in a parallel struggle. Paul watching his son play soccer is experiencing his own differentiation. His identity as a "younger man," or perhaps even as the fantasized "hero" within his own life, is changing; he's beginning to accept himself as a more mature, middle-aged man. Thanks to his involvement with his son, he's vicariously rediscovering the circular, transitional, and changing nature of his own life's journey, recognizing the painful losses, frightening changes, and exciting opportunities for growth that persist no matter how old we are.

Paul's profound experience of seeing himself as a progenitor—

father of a new generation—is crucial to how he navigates the later phases of his own adult development: his midlife, late life, and old age. In this way, while Paul is developing as a father, helping Mark master the task of growing up, Paul's own development is influenced and shaped by the demands fatherhood places upon him.

By staying engaged with their sons, men can learn to come to grips with their own limitations, both as men and as fathers, and become better able to differentiate themselves from their self-images as younger men. They can also achieve a deeper understanding of, and oftentimes a fuller reconciliation with, their own fathers.

Many men find it difficult to admit to themselves their own failures as men. Until middle age, they went through life thinking of themselves as somewhat heroic, whether this conception is linked to their success at work, their capacities as a member of a family, or perhaps to achievements and conquests prior to settling down. Experiencing their sons' disdain, they often begin to question their own heroic stature, to consider their disappointments and thwarted ambitions. However painful, this kind of reflection can ultimately lead a man to create a more realistic and durable self-image.

THE IMPORTANCE OF EXPERIENCING ADOLESCENT INDIVIDUATION

Gratifications and disappointments for the father exist throughout his son's development. However, they usually peak during adolescence, as the child begins to distance and remove himself from his family dependencies. The ebbing of the most active period of parenting is heralded by the multiple changes taking place. Fathers need to mourn as the son's "second individuation" transpires, while simultaneously experiencing gratification in the son's push toward independence. A father's identification with his son renders this particular differentiation more likely because, in vicariously reliving his own adolescent challenges, he has an opportunity to rework some of the disappointments and ambitions of his own youth while steering his son toward a more realistic concept of self. By helping to guide their teenage sons, fathers frequently recall and often relive their own adolescent triumphs and pitfalls, only now with the benefit of adult hindsight. Lasting feelings of self-consciousness and diminished self-worth stemming from their own teenage years can be placed in perspective, once and for all, as fathers recognize their sons' unique struggles in this domain and assist their boys to manage these issues with some levelheadedness. Feelings of impotence, loss, and resignation are nonetheless inevitable as fathers gradually abandon the role as father to a "young boy."

The boy's task during this second major stage of defining himself is to achieve what psychoanalysts call "adult genital desire" whereby an adult capacity for intimacy is forged. He also consolidates his gender identity and object choice (i.e., female or male), and strives to acquire the ego maturation and stabilization of interests that derive from the loss and mourning involved in disengaging from his more infantile relationship to his parents. As I've indicated, the father is idealized in pre- and early adolescence as his son's non-erotic, protective yearnings are revived, while by mid-adolescence, this same father is undervalued as his son seeks to break from his childhood. A father who can appreciate his adolescent son's developmental task fosters his boy's ability to increasingly relinquish his infantile, preambivalent, idealizing attachment needs in order to form an adult ego ideal.

This permits the teenage son to integrate his early, pre-oedipal relationship to his father, and in turn, facilitates the son's ability to venture toward the outside, adult world in a primarily non-conflicted way.[5]

The father must also bear his son's disillusionment and painful deidealization. Just as he once actively contributed to his son's identification with him (and an optimal distancing from the mother), the father now must engage, but in a more passive or peripheral way, with his son's gradual and repetitive differentiation from him. Fathers are moreover called upon to support with interested restraint their sons' experimentation with new identities, as well as their engagement with "substitute" fathers who often stand in stark opposition. Fathers' consistency, integrity, and healthy narcissism are crucial in this respect.

EXPERIMENTATION WITHIN LIMITS

Boys at this stage seem irresistibly drawn to experimentation, to test boundaries and limits. At times, such adolescent behavior is often intentionally provocative in that the parents' disapproval reinforces a boy's separateness from his parents. Nonetheless, fathers must keep in mind that however far the risk-taking adolescent will go, he does *not* want to harm himself or destroy his place in the family.

The father of a teenage boy is constantly challenged to understand that these provocations, such as getting drunk or taking drugs, dating girls known for their skimpy outfits, joining a cult, or hiding behind cynicism, are all expressions of the boy's yearning to try on new identities. There's a "just practicing" quality to all these behaviors that is reminiscent of when these sons were toddlers—they'd inch away from Mom, one step at a time, until they suddenly discovered they were too far away and with fear in their eyes, would scurry back to her. Similarly, teenagers experiment with their evolving selves while eschewing a permanent commitment to anything. Fathers are called upon to recognize their son's unique individuality, while walking a very fine line between overreacting (thereby encouraging the son to become even more dangerously rebellious and pull further away in his efforts to define himself), and in contrast, ignoring the provocation (leaving their son to feel overwhelmed and abandoned by a father who seems to be missing-in-action). In short, they need to support their son's experimentation, within reasonable limits, even while disapproving of the specific activities. In setting reasonable limits, fathers will be particularly helpful in translating a teenage boy's proclivity to act out his feelings rather than talk about them.

For example, Frank consulted me about his seventeen-year-old son, Jerry. They had always had a close relationship, but recently, Jerry had become unruly and verbally combative with his father. I helped Frank deal with his difficulty in bearing his son's belligerence and instead, learn to establish firm, constructive limits that would help Jerry with his own tendency to act out his feelings.

One evening after Frank told Jerry that he couldn't use the family car, Jerry simply grabbed the car keys and headed toward the garage. Frank was livid but tried to remain in control, reflecting on what he and I had discussed about setting reasonable limits and finding ways to help his son translate his actions into more civilized expression. He told me how he stood in front of Jerry and stated firmly that he needed to stop going any further. Frank then said, "You cannot have the car tonight. I don't care how angry you are with me, you still have to watch what you say and do. I won't tolerate your cursing at me, treating your mother or me as if we have no feelings, or defying rules and standards in our home."

Jerry didn't reply as he tossed the keys to the ground and scuffled back to his room, but neither did he have an outburst like that again. Though Frank was far from being able to acknowledge it to himself, I helped him to realize that like most teenagers, Jerry was actually begging for his father to set some limits for him, and on this particular occasion, to keep him home that evening.

Once Frank established this ground rule, he no longer feared that Jerry would verbally abuse him, and father and son began to talk more honestly. "I understand you don't appreciate some things that I do," Frank told Jerry one night as they cleared the table, "and you can politely criticize them if you like, and I'll try to listen." Because Frank wasn't defensive, Jerry felt more inclined to open up. He was still distant, but at least he was more respectful as he began to talk about why he felt so angry at home. As for Frank, he was learning to channel his own helpless feelings into constructive actions by establishing necessary and appropriate limits for his teenage son. Frank's ability to tolerate his son's more restrained expression of his devaluing impulses helped Jerry to integrate his own difficult, conflicting feelings about his father in a constructive fashion.

DIFFERENTIATING FROM FATHERS

Boys who are unable, for various reasons, to undergo this phase of deidealization and devaluation of their fathers often encounter problems later in life. Some go through life with a consistently idealized picture of their fathers, rigidly defending them without backing down; conversely, they may endlessly devalue and blame their fathers, unable to feel any compassion. However the scenario plays out, it leaves men fixated on an unrealistic sense of their fathers and themselves, and consequently, it leaves boys unable fully to mature.

Jeffrey, for instance, grew up in a small Midwestern town, the only son of the town's highly respected and much-loved pediatrician. His father unexpectedly died from a massive heart attack when Jeffrey was fifteen years old; later, his mother began openly to denigrate his father. Jeffrey went on to excel at an Ivy League college but subsequently dropped out of graduate school. He pursued a variety of careers, including the priesthood, engineering, and the law. Each pursuit resulted, however, in his stopping just short of finishing his degree or earning his final credential (for example, he failed the bar exam several times).

Jeffrey began treatment with me as a married thirty-five-year-old with two small children. His latest career was failing and his marriage was floundering. He was very depressed, plagued by self-doubts, and concerned about increasing homosexual fantasies. He remained very close to but highly critical of his mother, while experiencing considerable conflict and isolation from his father-in-law. All the while, Jeffrey clung tenaciously to a romantic and idealistic picture of his father as the "perfect man."

Within six months, Jeffrey became quite involved in our work together and his external life began to improve. Soon thereafter, however, he became extremely critical of the treatment and easily upset with me. "Everyone agrees that I haven't made any progress here," he said, referring to his wife, mother, and father-in-law. "They want to know what I plan to do with my life. Time's running out."

Soon after this conversation, during one session he became

enraged at me. He started shouting, his face turned red, and for a moment I thought he was going to pick up a paperweight and hurl it at me. Over the course of the next few sessions, his attacks on me became so ruthless that I had to struggle to stay in my role as therapist. In fact, I had to work hard to understand and endure my own feelings as he attacked me. The retaliatory anger that he provoked in me is what psychoanalysts call "countertransference," and I was certainly being tested as to whether I could keep mine in check.

What helped me maintain a therapeutic distance during these assaults on me was my realization that he was treating me this way because our present-tense relationship was a mirror of a past inner relationship that Jeffrey had never worked out. In his eyes, I'd become just like his "perfect" father, and he wished for and expected things from me—and from himself—that couldn't possibly be realized. As a result, he felt bitterly disappointed and furious, experiencing me as a betrayer who led him to think that I had the answers but who, instead, was really just a "con." He therefore was ultimately trying to get rid of me, a "flawed" and worthless entity, as quickly as possible.

When he calmed down and we finally were able to talk about what had happened, he admitted that this was the first time he'd ever been able directly to express his rage and disappointment at a man who was trying to take care of him. He gradually came to experience the necessary process of deidealization and optimal differentiation from a father he saw "on a pedestal." His father's narcissistic needs and inability to tolerate his son's disillusionment, coupled with his sudden death and Jeffrey's mother's abrupt denigration of a revered father, had interfered with Jeffrey's forming an adult ego ideal. Jeffrey could neither mourn his loss in disengaging from the idealized father of his childhood, nor move into mature manhood without a father capable of bearing his own deidealization and, subsequently, facilitating his son's integrated, mature masculinity. Also, because Jeffrey had the sense that his father couldn't have abided Jeffrey's dissatisfaction with him, I became the first man in his life with whom he dared to "lose it." Once Jeffrey could appreciate the meaning of his disillusionment and anger, our work progressed.

In short, those adolescent boys fortunate enough to have a father who can bear being pushed off his pedestal often end up feeling freer to identify with selected aspects of their fathers rather than the whole. This, in turn, eventually enables them to modify their own desired, often perfectionist ideals so that their depictions of themselves become more realistic and flexible. These boys are more able to experience themselves as having both strengths and weaknesses, much like their own fathers, and thus, can judge themselves more realistically as they venture out into their grown-up lives, aware of their own strengths and limitations.

FATHERS AND SONS COPING WITH LOSS

Underlying all the feelings that get churned up during adolescence—excitement, rage, disequilibrium, joy, fear, isolation, and even ecstasy—is the feeling of loss. As Raymond Carver writes in his short story "Bicycles, Muscles, Cigarettes":

> The boy rolled onto his side and watched his father walk to the door . . . and then the boy said, "Dad? You'll think I'm pretty crazy, but I wish I'd known you when you were . . . about as old as I am right now. I don't know how to say it, but I'm lonesome about it. It's like—it's like I miss you

already if I think about it now. That's pretty crazy, isn't it?"[6]

The grown-up world has proven to many boys to be as frightening as it is tantalizing. In fact, they oftentimes act defiant precisely because they're fearful. Teenage boys, at least those raised in relatively stable families, mourn many losses: closeness with parents; their perception of their parents as healthy and youthful; their own sense of themselves as children; their familiar boyhood bodies; the conviction that the world is safe and dependable; and innocence itself. Judith Viorst, a writer and psychoanalyst, writes that teenagers are set down "on the shore of a turbulent sea" where they plainly see that "leaving could mean drowning." Many intuit that their sense of loss and sadness will only intensify with time. In Viorst's words, "the gates of Eden are clanging shut for good."[7]

Some boys are unable to accept this necessary mourning. They defend themselves against loss by prolonging their adolescence. Others try to cling to childhood by regressing: they throw tantrums as they did when they were toddlers, get sick frequently so they can stay home and not go to school, detach themselves socially, appear withdrawn, or become so irresponsible that they, in effect, demand extra parental attention and adult supervision.

A father can help in his son's grieving process by acknowledging his son's losses while supporting the gains that growing older confers. For instance, Zack, the fifteen-year-old son of an acquaintance, who had always been an excellent student, saw his grades plummet during his sophomore year of high school. He refused to do homework, objecting to it on philosophical grounds, never studied for tests, and failed to hand in even the homework and lab reports he'd actually completed. His parents were unable to influence Zack to work harder in school and asked me for the name of a therapist. I referred them to a family therapist who wisely suggested that Zack's school performance was in fact his way of expressing his unhappiness over growing older. Zack was dragging his academic feet because he was terrified about being on a path leading to college, which meant leaving home, a separation for which he wasn't emotionally prepared.

Recognizing that the issue was emotional rather than academic, Zack's father lightened up on the subject of grades. And once he no longer felt academic pressure from his parents, Zack felt freer to voice his apprehension about leaving home. When he could directly address his fears, Zach no longer needed to act out at school; in a matter of months, his average began to improve. Zack still experienced many ambivalent feelings about growing up, but they became easier to manage with his father's help. Together, they talked about the challenges of growing up. In experiencing his father's understanding and willingness to stay involved with him emotionally, Zack was no longer dominated by his unspoken fears.

Fathers of teenage boys also feel the same mounting sense of loss and emptiness. Fathers who know they are slowly being phased out of their sons' lives, who sense that they are no longer the center of their sons' universe, experience tremendous sadness and hurt, just as Paul did when he reflected that all he was to his son these days was a chauffeur. But Paul was also mourning his own lost youth. Watching his strong son sprint down the soccer field, Paul found himself lost in nostalgia, remembering his own days on his high school football team, when he could catch a pass and elude tacklers with ease. He still felt as if he could break out in a run, but he knew that if he did, he'd end up breathing hard, pull a hamstring, and feel foolish. Yet what he'd lost in vigor and stamina, he'd gained in terms of his new understanding of life—that we all inevitably move from one stage to the next, and that loss and gain are inextricably intertwined.

Fathers also suffer additional momentous losses during this phase of development. In fact, middle age is a particularly evocative time for them. Vicariously identifying with their sons' budding sexuality, many fathers are pulled back into their own pasts, reliving former triumphs and awkward pitfalls during their "wonder years." Some men go so far as to act out these feelings, beginning affairs with younger women, for instance. Midlife crises like these, acted out by men desperately trying to hold onto their own youthful image, have unfortunately become a culture cliché.

As proud as they are of their sons, other feelings such as envy inevitably get stirred up. It's often very hard for some men, who see their waist size increasing and their hairline receding, to catch glimpses of their teenage sons' taut stomachs and muscular limbs, to say nothing of the girls they bring home as compared to aging wives. However, this is not the first time men have envied their sons. Many felt it when their sons were only infants and had their mothers all to themselves. But in those early days, a father's envy abated when he identified with his infant son and formed his own unique bond with him. At this stage of development, the son is moving away from his father, not closer to him. As a result, the father's envy often grows more intense. Unable to bond with his son, who is becoming more sexual as well as more distant, the father is left to bear his feelings alone, fated to watch his child turn into a "young man" while he himself becomes an "old man." This may be the first time that men experience their own and their sons' lives diverging instead of coming together.

Men who can recognize and contain their grief and envious feelings—especially in the face of increasing separation from their sons—and take responsibility for them allow their sons to grow up feeling more positively about their own identity and sexuality. Similarly, those men who learn to experience the sting of their sons' differentiation constructively—who neither turn against their sons nor become unduly self-critical, morose, and withdrawn because of their sons' dismissal—will reap further emotional closeness and personal satisfaction in years to come, and will also discover that they have come to understand their own competitive feelings, jealousy, loss, and very sense of identity in novel and complex ways.

For example, Brad, a fifty-three-year-old patient, initially described himself as tremendously proud of his seventeen-year-old son, Jayson. However, as we began exploring his deeper feelings, he was in considerable pain because he resented Jayson's apparent ease in excelling both academically and socially. Colleges were actively courting Jayson, and each time he came home with another piece of good news, Brad felt himself cringing inside.

Brad had recently learned that he would require hip-replacement surgery and his business was doing poorly. Despite these personal setbacks, he couldn't understand why he was reacting so negatively to his son's successes, and yet he knew that he needed to keep his resentful feelings under control.

Brad increasingly felt more comfortable talking about these feelings with me and indicated fearing that his own best days were behind him. He told me that he loved his son and didn't want to harm him, yet he couldn't keep his resentment, anger, and fear of infirmity and growing old from surfacing.

Over time, as he revealed his feelings and concerns to me, he began to experience some relief. As we discussed the difficulties inherent in seeing his son on such a smooth ascent while he felt himself so in decline, he told me: "You seem to understand my feelings and apparently don't see them as so unnatural." It helped Brad to know that he wasn't the only father who harbored ambivalent feelings about an individuating son's triumphs in conjunction with his own setbacks. Our work helped him to realize that his challenge would be to accept that his feelings, however uncomfortable, belonged to him, and that he had to simply experience them without acting them out destructively. Moreover, they didn't have to prevent him from being a good father. Eventually, Brad was able to take pride in the fact that he was protecting his son from unnecessary manifestations of his own pain.

By the end of adolescence, a boy has reached a momentous milestone: childhood's end. If all has gone well, he has established a new identity that's both flexible and stable. He feels empowered to make choices, relying more upon his own judgment. He's more comfortable with his masculinity, having integrated into it some qualities typically considered feminine, and he has also essentially accepted his sexual orientation. Perhaps he's even come to terms with traumatic events in his childhood and is finally beginning to figure out how to forgive his parents for whatever wrongs they might have done him over the years, at least for the most part. The older adolescent has achieved a sense of historical continuity with the past, and is starting to internalize a more realistic picture of himself that includes values and commitments related to his place in the wider world.

His father is also closer to resolving his parallel issues pertaining to identity, differentiation, and loss. He's ceded the "heroic quest" to his son, and has found ways to face the years ahead with a new understanding of mortality. Now it's time for young men to begin their adult lives, and for fathers to face up to this fact in addition to the reality of their own aging, as I shall discuss in the remaining chapters.

7

COACHING FROM THE SIDELINES

To be a man is, precisely, to be responsible.

—ANTOINE DE SAINT-EXUPÉRY[1]

My colleague Wes has a son named Eli, who had just graduated from college when I was told this story. Eli's plan for the coming year was to rent an apartment in town, get a job as a cook, and apply to engineering graduate school for the following semester. It sounded good on paper, but things started to go wrong almost immediately. First, the friend with whom Eli was planning on renting an apartment got a job offer overseas, leaving Eli scrambling to find a new roommate before the rent was due. Then, the restaurant where Eli was working got hit by lightning a week after it opened. Eli, along with most of the newly hired staff, was let go, only to find that most of the other viable jobs were already taken.

That's when Eli called Wes. "I want to come home, Dad," he told his father. "I can't take it living here. The kid I'm living with now never locks his door, and won't take out the garbage. He spends every night with his girlfriend hooking up on the living-room couch, which means I'm stuck in my room. I can't find a job. I don't know what I'm doing here."

Wes heard his son's anguish. In many ways, he told me, all he wanted to say to his son was, "Sure, come on home. You'll find a job here, and we'll take care of you." But he knew that wouldn't help Eli in the long run.

So he took a deep breath and said, "I think you should stay where you are. You'll find a job; you just have to keep looking. As for your roommate, tell him that if he doesn't start acting more responsibly, you'll find someone else. Neither task will be easy, but I have faith in you."

"You don't know what you're talking about!" Eli exploded. "There are no jobs. I can't believe you're making me stay here. You mean I can't even come home for the weekend?"

"Of course you can come home for the weekend, but then you'll have to go back," Wes said. "Think about it. Do you really want to live at home with your mother and me?"

Eli sighed audibly, and with great sadness. "Sometimes, Dad, I'm not sure what I want," he said.

On the brink of adulthood, young men need to begin to create an autonomous life where they can experience themselves as adult men able to function independently, apart from their families. This entails two tasks: finding their place in the world (which includes creating a career direction); and forming intimate, lasting love relationships. Neither is easy. Gail Sheehy uses the term "turbulent twenties" to refer to this developmental stage when many young men find themselves facing a bewildering array of choices without the benefit of any clear road map.[2] Fathers, for their part, have to assume yet another new role with their sons. Although their relationship is often warm and loving, free of the competitive and sexual tensions that may have dogged them in the past, the power differential has irrevocably changed. Until now, the father-son relationship was based in an inequity. Now, as the son ascends to adulthood, the relationship slowly changes to one between equals, or peers, though the older partner is naturally more experienced.

Unsure of what role to take, fathers need to adapt to long-distance fathering in which they withhold judgment and leave much of the direct mentoring to other older men. However, because they may be summoned at any time to help their sons venture further into the adult world, fathers need to remain poised and ready on the sidelines to step in at a moment's notice.

BREAKING AWAY . . . AGAIN

Young men like Eli need to complete what developmental theorists refer to as the "third individuation." Aware of the fact that they are responsible for taking the next series of steps into maturity, they work hard to distance themselves from the protective parental orbit and their childhood selves in order to create their own sense of adult identity.[3] Daniel Levinson, a research psychologist and the primary investigator of a comprehensive empirical study of adult men's development, characterizes these young men as "novice adults."[4] There's a provisional quality to them, as if they're apprenticing at establishing a mature male identity. Their center of gravity has shifted; they no longer locate themselves in their families of origin, but they have not yet fully established a home base of their own. The independence they claim is often more illusory than real, and many still depend on their parents for financial as well as emotional support.

At the same time, a young man in his twenties begins to articulate for himself what Levinson calls a "personal dream." That is, he tries to envision his role in the world of adults while figuring out who he is and what he wants to accomplish in his life. This awareness of the potential within him, of the man he could become, generates excitement and vitality, helping to propel him into adulthood. Frequently, drawing on the skills he mastered as a teenager, he becomes preoccupied with crafting a public image of himself that showcases his skills and talents: an "outer self" or "persona" on which he relies to win success and approval in the world. Oftentimes driven by a need to become a "hero" in the eyes of his peers, colleagues, and in his own estimation, he seeks to excel and achieve, sometimes at any cost.

A father helps his son craft this personal dream by supporting it. Often this means that the older man vicariously identifies with and affirms the young man's voyage of discovery. In turn, the father has to relinquish his own vision of himself as a hero, thereby passing the torch of heroism down to his son. Many men, in fact, glimpsed the beginning of this process years ago at their son's birth when they found themselves focusing more so on their child's trajectory than their own.

All young men, no matter how rebellious or independent they may seem, desire their fathers' approbation. They want to know that they are recognized and appreciated for their own manhood as well as for their uniquely constructed identity. The task of forming a commitment to a career and to a lasting intimate relationship is the primary challenge for young men; yet their struggles in these two domains frequently cause them to feel immature, inadequate, and unmanly. Consequently, particularly when a young man is floundering and feels ashamed, he seeks his father's assurance that his problematical efforts to establish an adult identity don't compromise his manhood.

But a father's approval is significant for another reason. When a young man feels his father's respect, he can continue to successfully deidealize his father, a process that began in late adolescence. In other words, when a young man feels his father's support, he has no need to worship his father; he can take back some of the power he projected onto his father and claim it as his own.

Consider L. Frank Baum's novel *The Wonderful Wizard of Oz*.[5] Dorothy's three male companions—a cowardly Lion, a brainless Scarecrow, and a heartless Tin Man—are depicted as grown men in dire need of male mentoring to free themselves from the perpetual childhood in which they are stuck. Together with the residents of the Emerald City, they create an idealized image of a wise and wonderful mentor or father figure: the Wizard of Oz. Ultimately, he is revealed to be merely an ordinary man, but not before he helps the three travelers uncover and then affirm their own underdeveloped courage, brain, and heart respectively, which are all qualities necessary to secure their passage into manhood. The Wizard then generously accepts his own deidealization when the three travelers reveal him as a sham. As the story illustrates, when young men reclaim some of the power they attributed to their fathers, they are able to achieve a more realistic, mature, and integrated sense of their own manhood.

· · ·

A NEW STYLE OF MENTORING

Sometimes, however, fathers need to mentor their sons from the sidelines, conferring their blessings while not actively offering advice. Danny, a young man of twenty-five, came to see me because he felt "stuck"; he saw all of his friends as being more "grown-up" than he was. Although he wanted to take the next step into adulthood, he kept finding himself distracted. "There's this woman at work," he explained. "She's incredibly sexy and I think about her all the time. She likes me too, I can tell. I know if I got things on with her, it would jeopardize my situation at work and it would really hurt my girlfriend if she ever found out. But maybe she wouldn't find out, and sometimes I don't even *care* if she finds out. My body wants this other woman so much that I'm close to just giving in to my urges."

When I asked Danny what he wanted, he said that he wished that an "authority figure"—such as George, his mentor at the company—would tell him that he was "stupid" to even think of acting on his lust, and that he shouldn't give in to temptation but should instead start thinking about what's really important to him.

"It sounds to me as if you know what to do," I said.

Danny nodded in agreement, but insisted that "It's just so much easier if someone else is the authority who tells me what to do, because then I can just be responsible for whether or not I follow their directions. It's a lot harder to be responsible for *myself*, to pay attention to what I know inside and then follow it."

Clearly, what Danny wanted from me was a "father's blessing," since his own father had died five years earlier. He needed me to affirm his nascent yet burgeoning internal sense of authority.

I empathized with his struggle, knowing full well that to be fully human requires wrestling with this very issue throughout one's life. Every man must find a rapprochement between his impulses and his more developed mental functions. Particularly for a young man, achieving further resolution of this struggle is essential to establish his own niche in the world.

I asked Danny if he had a fantasy of what he'd like to do with his life as an adult. He spoke passionately for about twenty minutes about the life he envisioned for himself. I then asked if he thought that acting on his desires for this attractive woman at work would have a negative impact on his plan. He thought about this for a moment, and then replied that it surely would.

In this way, I helped Danny to use his "dream" to recognize that, as an adult, he was capable of paving his own way and making his own decisions; having a goal for which to strive ultimately enhanced his ability to listen to himself. In the end, he was able to access the authority figure within, and thereby become more comfortable with the choices and necessary losses involved in following the road to becoming a responsible adult man. This anecdote illustrates how important it is for a father or mentor to hold back or contain his own desires to act as *the* authority, a role he had once assumed with his son, and instead encourage and facilitate the young man's discovery that he is, in fact, his *own* personal authority. Only then can this young man break away from his mentor to become an individual who is confident in his autonomy as well as in his ability to make decisions.

ENABLING SONS TO BREAK AWAY

Some fathers struggle to accept their sons' decisions for how they wish to structure their adult lives. Isaac, for example, who'd had a very successful career in investment banking, came to see me to talk about his concerns for his twenty-four-year-old son Dave. Throughout college and graduate school, Dave had faithfully followed in his father's footsteps, majoring in business and interning at financial institutions every summer. Therefore, when without warning he announced that he'd changed his mind and wished to pursue a career as a jazz pianist, Isaac was crushed—and furious. "I'm not going to support you financially if you insist on following this crazy dream," Isaac would tell his son again and again.

"I'm not asking you for money," Dave always replied, but when each time he called and alluded to his impoverished state, Isaac could barely contain himself.

"When I was his age," he told his wife, "I was already working at the bank."

"No, you weren't," his wife said, gently reminding him that soon after his own graduation from college, Isaac set about to write a novel, moving back into his parents' house. He dithered away for two years with no money in his bank account and not even one chapter written; in fact, he didn't abandon his novel or bother to find a real job until the summer he got engaged.

When Isaac recounted this story to me, I delicately suggested that he tell it to his son. Though skeptical at first, he agreed, and at our next appointment he told me how well it had gone over. By remembering and reclaiming his own idealistic interlude, and by acknowledging his own vulnerability, Isaac was able to empathize with his son. He also no longer felt humiliated or personally rejected by his son's decision to do something admittedly risky with his life. Dave, in turn, recognized his father's appreciation for his unorthodox efforts to construct a unique adult identity.

Our consultations helped Isaac to understand that his son needed to follow his own dream. Isaac could set limits—he could refuse to send Dave money, for instance—but he could also try to support his son's dreams while at the same time taking responsibility for his own disappointments and fears. According to Judith Viorst, "Letting our children go, and letting our dreams for our children go, must be counted among our necessary losses."[6] That is, fathers need to not only let their young adult sons stake out their own directions but to let them be, and accept that their own wishes and their sons' decisions won't always coincide.

This is not the first time a father needs to let go of his needs in order to accede to another's It happened during his son's infancy when he had to relinquish his position as his wife's primary other, thus freeing her to nurture their infant son. It happened again in adolescence, when he had to let go of his own lofty, idyllic status as his son's hero while the boy experimented with new identities and found other men to admire and idealize. What's different about this juncture is that the father has to finally come to terms with who his son really is, what identity he has ultimately settled upon, and how he has decided to live his life.

An older man who blesses the younger man's adult choices levels the playing field so that each can better recognize the fact that they are equals as men, even though they differ in terms of their experiences. In part, this requires a father to open up to his son about his own young adulthood struggles, mistakes, and weaknesses as Isaac did. The father who can do so frees his son from the unrealistic and often suffocating burden of trying to live up to a rigid and constraining ideal of adult manhood. Indeed, it's through such intimate exchanges that both father and son help each other along in their development as adult men and open the door to a more mature relationship.

Both men learn important lessons about themselves during this phase of development. When Dave and Isaac were estranged, for example, Dave realized that he could tolerate his father's disappointment. In a sense, a young man leaves home emotionally when he stops seeing the world through the eyes of his parents. As Gail Sheehy puts it, "Prolonged adolescence ends, finally, when we are not afraid to disappoint our parents."[7]

At the same time, a father has to acknowledge himself as an aging, fallible, less-than-ideal parent. He needs to let go of his own fantasies about himself as perhaps being a better parent than he actually is. Every father harbors fantasies that he has raised an extraordinary son who will become a great scholar, a respected physician, a powerful and wealthy businessman, or perhaps even president. Moreover, the father imagines that his son's great achievements will reflect radiantly back onto him. This phase of life, however, is when these fantasies collide with an often jarring reality. A father has to accept that his influence over the trajectory of his son's life is over. The younger man's future is his own; he alone is now responsible for what happens to him. All that fathers can do is hope their sons are well enough prepared to meet that future and the challenges along the way.

FOSTERING A CAPACITY FOR INTIMACY

A young man's other important task, in addition to settling on a vocation, is to find and sustain intimate relationships. As Erik Erikson reminds us, a young man's primary crisis is one of intimacy versus isolation—that is, he either begins establishing himself in intimate relationships or risks becoming isolated.[8] An intimate couple requires two firmly established selves, while *mature intimacy* requires that both people feel sufficiently secure with their personal boundaries to allow the other person to slip inside his or her protective covering. Intimate relating proceeds when both people desire to become closer while maintaining their own sense of self, a development that requires the ability to recognize the objective existence of another while simultaneously acknowledging the other's subjective experience as being equally valid to one's own. This plays out in sexual relations, when young men find themselves asked to focus more on attaining mutual satisfaction than on achieving pleasure only for themselves. Intimacy also depends on one's ability to make sacrifices or compromises, and to risk being seen as vulnerable. This is often a difficult task for men, as they are typically socialized to shy away from such openness lest they be viewed as not sufficiently masculine.

Fathers can help their sons find meaningful, intimate relations with others by modeling these kinds of relationships with other adults, including their sons. A father who supports his son's self-sufficiency and unique sense of manhood paves the way for the younger man to achieve adult intimacy with others.

Dave, the aspiring jazz musician, saw how hard his father was working to accept and support his career path in both word and deed. Isaac talked to his friends about Dave's talent and progress, and came to see him perform at various clubs. As Dave felt more supported, he began to value his father again as a model of a mature man, one who is able to reach out to others despite conflicts and differences, without giving up his own sense of self. When Dave met a woman he liked and began to date seriously, he relied on his relationship with his dad as well as what he had always observed between his mother and father as models for a close and healthy relationship.

Young men who do not have fathers to both model and reflect the capacity for intimate relationships often shy away from intimacy. Some men who have been deficient in such fathering tend to eschew couple relationships altogether, whereas others often engage in a promiscuous pseudo-intimacy by compulsively seeking new and desirable love affairs. When a man cannot achieve true intimacy with a partner, he tends to feel deeply isolated in a solipsistic world of his own creation. Such was the case with Ben, a twenty-nine-year-old movie executive. A self-described "sex addict," he felt that his identity was defined by the number of women he'd slept with—approximately two hundred, he proudly told me—as well as the size of his penis, which he described as "so huge, most women just can't resist." Though extremely successful financially, Ben felt "lost" and isolated in his huge house, "bored" with his work, and imagined himself ending up "alone and deranged." Beneath the gregarious and manic veneer, Ben was a tragically sad and lost young man by the time he came to see me.

I learned that Ben was estranged from his father, Nick, a philanderer and alcoholic. Ben recalled the many painful hours he had spent at home with his mother and brother waiting for his dad to return from one of his regular evenings out. Although Ben loved his father, he cringed whenever he saw the way his dad treated his mom. As the years passed, Nick's evenings out increased, and by the time the boys were teenagers, he rarely spoke to Ben and his brother other than to say something along the lines of "You guys remember, work hard because you've got only yourself to rely on."

Ben went to college and studied hard; in his free time, he got high smoking pot. After graduation, he landed an excellent job in a major Los Angeles film studio, and recalled having his "mind blown" by both the number of attractive women surrounding him and the cornucopia of intoxicants available to him. He couldn't bear being alone, yet seemed unable to form a meaningful relationship with a woman. In time, he began abusing substances and sleeping around.

Initially, Ben approached therapy as if it were an opportunity to dump his problems and get rid of his frustrations so that he simply could be freer to pursue his conquests. For my part, I admit it was often difficult to sit with him as he performed his manic monologues and strutted his stuff. I realized, however, how much he needed me to be a firm male presence precisely because his very identity and sense of masculinity were in a state of arrested development. We persevered, and over the course of a year, as he began to trust me more, I could more directly confront him about his behavior. I tried to help him understand its underlying meaning, particularly how it related to his search for a realistic adult male presence in his life and his longing for a father to recognize his wounds and guide him.

As if Ben was an adolescent and I his father, I steadfastly challenged his destructive behavior, setting appropriate limits, and supporting his efforts to establish an identity and increase his capacity for intimacy. It was demanding work for both of us, but after several years and some risky episodes, Ben began to gain control over his addictions. He also became reflective enough that he could tolerate more meaningful conversation with me. In a sense, psychoanalytic therapy and Ben's adult life were just beginning.

YOUNG ADULT SONS INFLUENCING THEIR FATHERS

As we've seen in every previous phase of development, sons help their fathers grow, and that continues to be true even now that both father and son are adults. Sometimes, however, a father's growth comes with considerable pain, requiring him to confront himself in difficult ways. In my clinical work, I am reminded often that intimacy remains a problem for many older men as well as for their sons. For a father who thinks that expressing vulnerability isn't masculine, it's often his son who finds a way to break through those defenses and uncover the emotional man hiding within.

For instance, twenty-four-year-old Paolo, whose father became my patient in couples therapy, was devastated when his girlfriend broke up with him. Struggling with her rejection and unable to find a job he enjoyed, he became increasingly depressed and isolated. His parents knew nothing about it until the police called to report that Paolo had been in a car accident and arrested for a DUI. Paolo's father, Rafael, immediate flew across the country to bail out his terribly humiliated and by now despairing son.

Father and son lived together in Paolo's apartment for a week, spending more time together than they had in the last ten years. At first, Paulo refused to talk, but one night he utterly broke down. Rafael—a warm, seemingly self-assured man, although very controlled and doctrinaire—was frightened and initially angry with his "weak" son, whom he viewed as "too close to his mother." But his anger soon gave way to love and concern. Eventually, Rafael opened up too, comforting and sharing his own pain with his son. "Mom and I have struggled in our marriage for years, Paulo, as you may or may not know," he told his son. "It's been very hard and we've made some big mistakes. But we both love you and are here for you now. Just tell me what you need from me."

"Just you, Dad, I just need you!" Paolo replied.

Rafael's first impulse was to say, "But I've been here all along!" He thought of all the things they'd done together over the years—going on fishing trips, hiking in the mountains, doing carpentry together. Yet somewhere inside he knew that Paulo was asking for him to let his guard down, something that until this moment Rafael hadn't been able to offer.

"Son, I'm a proud man," Rafael began. "Maybe I haven't let you get close to me some ways. Come to think of it, I have trou-

ble letting anyone get close to me—that's what Mom's been saying for a long time. But to see you in such pain is very hard for
me. My pain? Well, it's there but I keep it at a distance by working hard, drinking wine every night, and just putting one foot in
front of the other. I think you are old enough now, and maybe I
am too, that I can tell you about it."

Rafael had never opened up that way to anyone. With tears in
their eyes, father and son embraced and talked for hours, sharing their disappointments in each other and in themselves. In the
end each felt comforted. Seeing how badly Paolo needed him as
he truly was, Rafael became more self-accepting—with all his
limitations, talents, flaws, abilities, weaknesses, and strengths. A
door had opened for this father and son that would never fully
close again.

For Rafael, as he later told me in couples therapy, it felt as if
that door was opening for the first time. In seeing that he'd bared
his essential self to Paolo, who in turn embraced rather than
rejected him, Rafael recognized that his son was offering him an
opportunity to escape from the self-imposed isolation and highly
confined, dronelike world in which he'd been living. Soon after
he returned home, Rafael approached his wife, Helen, and told
her that he was ready to begin couples therapy with her—something she'd been urging him to do for many years.

Rafael and Helen started their therapy fighting and crying; it
took them time to learn to stop shouting and listen to one
another. Gradually, Rafael began drinking less and his health
slowly improved, an important first step toward transforming
their marriage. There were no easy solutions, but for the first
time in decades, their relationship was beginning to come alive
again. A grateful Rafael felt that he was finally able to imagine
himself moving forward in his life with a sense of energy and purpose rather than succumbing to stagnation and bitterness.

• • •

The theme of a son's ability to heal a wounded father is an old one. In the Grail myth, a knight son's virtuous acts restore the king-fisher and his languishing kingdom. The writer and poet Phil Cousineau lends a contemporary perspective to this ancient theme that transcends a father's death:

> *For my father and all fathers*
> *Who never saw Paris,*
> *One friend listens, reveals,*
> *Reaches in an open wound,*
> *Finds a piece of gold shrapnel,*
> *Cashes it in for airfare,*
> *Takes his father to the Left Bank*
> *So the healing*
> *Can begin.*[9]

THE TIME FOR RECOGNITION

Sam Osherson once wrote that "Until a man 'names his father,' sees him clearly, and accepts him for who he is and was, it is that much more difficult for him to grow up himself and become a father to his children, a husband to his wife, or a mentor to the younger generation at work."[10] That is, for many men in their twenties, their quest for adulthood isn't complete until they are ready to see their fathers realistically, for who they truly are, and to accept them with all their strengths as well as their weaknesses, vulnerabilities, and so on.

Furthermore, a son's "finding" of his father is oftentimes a revelatory experience, as a young man differentiating from his father to form his own identity ultimately discovers that his character is inescapably similar to his father's. Many sons in the course of adulthood stumble upon the unexpected truth that they are very much like their fathers were. The opportunity to understand and embrace one's father requires good fortune and significant longevity. Sadly, such moments of recognition between sons and their fathers are not always possible. If a father has been absent or abandoned his son, then the gulf may be too wide and the distance too great for rapprochement. Sometimes, a father is simply not available as a result of his own emotional turmoil, illness, or death. Yet there are times when reconciliation can, in fact, transcend the grave.

Greg was twenty-five years old when he began therapy with me because he was feeling very frustrated about his career and confused about relationships. It quickly became apparent that he felt inadequate and ashamed that his life seemed to "amount to nothing." Greg was both isolated and depressed, and seemed terribly burdened by seeing his father as a broken, failed man.

I understood Greg to be a young man much in need of coming to terms with his father in order to take the next step in his own life. Though he saw himself as completely different from his father, he nonetheless gave the impression of being stuck in time. I wondered to myself whether this might be because his own self-image was unconsciously constructed in line with how he conceived of his father. While such an interpretation would have made no sense to Greg early in our work together, I did tell him that it would be helpful to discuss his relationship with his father and try to come to a deeper understanding of what kind of person his father was. Greg then mused about how Ron, his father, might have felt when *he* was twenty-five. Greg sadly described how Ron had gone off to fight in Vietnam when he was only twenty years old, returning three years later a somewhat broken and disillusioned young man. Greg was born when Ron was twenty-four, and from what Greg had been told, his father was very uninvolved and emotionally detached from his young son and wife. As the years went by, Ron became an alcoholic and often fought bitterly with his wife and coworkers. He would periodically leave home on binges with his old buddies, only to end up hospitalized at the Veterans Hospital to receive treatment for his depression and substance abuse.

When Greg was a seventeen-year-old high school senior, Ron died from liver disease related to his alcoholism. Not surprisingly, Greg's memories of his father were mostly negative: he recalled Ron's drinking alone in front of the television or going out to the garage to smoke pot, his angry explosions at home, his workplace and financial difficulties, and his many hospitalizations.

I sympathized with Greg's feelings, but at the same time, I was struck by his complete lack of empathy for his father. Several months into our work, I was aware of Greg's growing trust for me, and so I brought up the issue of his lack of concern for his father. He seemed taken aback and yet, when I asked him if he had any other memories, Greg told me about the time Ron had coached Greg's Pop Warner football team, took him quail hunting, and eventually talked to him about his war experiences and feelings about American politics. Despite his conscious presentation, there was much more of a connection with his father than Greg had allowed himself to recognize.

Now that Greg was struggling to find his own niche in life, he began to rake over many more of these memories, the good ones as well as the bad. He wanted to imagine what it must have been like for his dad, a quiet yet intelligent kid from a small town, drafted as a college sophomore to fight in a war he didn't understand, returning home angry and cynical to discover that only alcohol and marijuana could ease his pain. Imagining his loneliness and desperation, Greg was able to think about his father with compassion for the first time.

"I wish I could talk to him right now," Greg told me, sobbing. "I want to tell him that I think I can finally begin to understand what it must have been like for him because I've been feeling lost myself. I wish he could be here, maybe even guide me, tell me that I've got it pretty fucking good, sitting here talking to a therapist, finding out who I am, having my health, my friends, my future. I wish I could have helped him, too."

Eventually, he began to realize that he *could* help his father, if only in spirit. "I want to find myself," Greg told me. "I want to do something to carry on his name in a way he could be proud of. That way, I can help both of us."

Over the next few months, Greg felt compelled to unravel the enigma of his father, exploring his father's life in our sessions and outside, contacting relatives and friends of his father to garner as much information as possible. In trying to form a more complete and accurate picture of his father, Greg was trying to better understand himself. Soon he began talking about something changing inside of him. It was a change I was witnessing as well—he was becoming noticeably more patient with himself, and much calmer. "I feel like my dad's with me in a different way," he explained. "I don't picture him anymore as that broken and 'cut-off' drunk guy I remember so well, but more and more as a young man again, one with hope and spirit I know he once had so much of and tried to find again but couldn't." As this internal process of reconciliation continued, Greg was maturing before my eyes. Within a year, he'd found his way into a job he loved. When I heard from him several years later, he told me he was about to be married.

Young men like Greg, lacking fathers who can help initiate them into manhood, are powerfully, albeit unconsciously driven to discover more about their fathers in order to better understand themselves. The representation they carry inside of their fathers may be puzzling or overly one-dimensional (in negative or positive ways); yet whatever it is, it forms an essential piece of the depiction the young man has built of himself. Consequently, to pursue his own version of manhood and mature himself, a young man needs to better understand his father. This "naming the father" enables him to move forward to find his own niche, no longer unconsciously trying to *be* his father or reacting *against* him. It is often crucial for the emotional maturation of young men with absent or otherwise insufficient father figures to engage in this process, and, hopefully, come to terms with who their fathers are—and were.

For his part, the father of a young man must face his own failures in attending to his son's development. In turn, partially through vicariously identifying with his son's quest to establish himself firmly in adulthood, the father begins passing the mantle of male "heroism" to his grown son. Moreover, sons who are able to experience their fathers' encouragement for their uniqueness and enthusiasm toward work are more likely to establish a commitment to their career.

Though it may take longer than it did a generation or two ago, men in their "turbulent twenties" eventually find work, settle down, and go about pursuing their individual lives. The next big step—becoming fathers themselves—will color their lives, as well as the lives of their own fathers, as the journey they are taking together moves into a new dimension.

8

MAN TO MAN

When a father gives to his son, both laugh.
When a son gives to his father, both cry.

—YIDDISH PROVERB [1]

Simon, a friend of mine, once told me the story of the moment he became, in his own words, a "grown-up." His son Mitchell was only six days old when he had to be returned to the hospital, having developed what appeared to be a strange infection. As Simon and his wife anxiously awaited the test results to determine whether Mitchell would need a complete blood transfusion, Simon took a minute to phone his parents who lived close by. In a panic, he told them what was unfolding, hoping they'd have something comforting or wise to say.

"A blood infection?" his father asked. "How can such a young baby get a blood infection?" His mother sounded equally befuddled, suggesting that Simon discharge his son from the first-rate hospital and drive the baby to the pediatrician Simon had seen as a child.

"In that moment," Simon recalled, "I realized that my parents had no answers for me; they knew even less than I did. They had no idea how to handle this crisis. It was up to my wife and me. We alone were responsible to make the important decisions."

Not every man crosses the threshold to adulthood in such a dramatic fashion, but most may begin to suspect, sometime during their thirties, that they've finally "grown up." According to Daniel Levinson, during the "age thirty transition," which occurs roughly between the ages of twenty-eight and thirty-three, a man realizes that the provisional, preparatory quality of the life he lived during his twenties is over—he is no longer a beginner, but "his own man."[2] Seeking success, he speaks more clearly with his own voice and commands a greater measure of authority. With the psychological separation from his parents complete, the stakes are raised: it's time to establish his position in the work world and to anchor himself and his family to society.

Additionally, whereas father and son often found themselves at cross-purposes in the past, they now discover that they are traveling on parallel tracks and that they actually have much in common. Both are engaged in the same, somewhat altruistic tasks, letting go of their own heroic dreams in order to advance the dreams and ambitions for their children. While the younger man focuses on his relationship with his own young children, his father is engaged in fostering "generativity." This term, coined by Erikson, refers to a man's desire to influence future generations—whether by having children on his own or by engaging in future-oriented work—and leave a legacy that survives him.[3] When an older man considers this idea, he is not dwelling on his lost youth, but rather is acknowledging that it is in his interest to help his progeny to achieve full adulthood. In this way, he also eases his fears about his own mortality.

RECIPROCALLY MATURING MASCULINITY

As men age, they often find themselves caring less and less about what society deems "manly." Their relentless need to achieve, so long construed as the defining element of masculinity, abates. As they abandon culturally bound distinctions of what is masculine and feminine, they feel freer to draw on their more nurturing and tender qualities. Often, they begin to resolve the polarities in their own psyches, reconciling the split not only between masculinity and femininity but also between creativity and destructiveness, as well as attachment and separation. Moreover, their sons often help them with this new acceptance.

Arthur, a thirty-nine-year-old, hard-driving, Type A corporate executive, began therapy with me because of "minor" problems in his marriage. Nonetheless, it was difficult to get a sense of his pain during our first several months because he presented himself as if he didn't need anyone, least of all me. In our fourth month together, his father, Everett, suffered an unexpected, life-threatening heart attack. After coronary bypass surgery, the sixty-six-year-old Everett retired from the publishing company where he'd worked for forty years. Arthur had always regarded his father as a pinnacle of strength; however, he now found himself concerned as much about his father's frame of mind as about his physical health. Although Everett recovered well from the operation, it seemed to have left deep psychological scars. "I feel as if I can't make decisions," he confided in his son. "I'm hesitant to do anything without your mother."

Although he tried to be supportive, Arthur found himself distressed by his father's new fearfulness. "He's become a wuss," Arthur told me. "I can't stand seeing him this way." I encouraged Arthur to examine what his father's vulnerabilities meant to him, and in reflecting over many sessions, Arthur ultimately began to consider his own anxieties. He revealed his fears of his father's death, and of dying himself; in addition, Arthur worried about becoming too dependent on his own wife.

Over the next several months, we started exploring what he referred to as his "hidden self." "Both my father and I seem to have buried our vulnerabilities deep inside the unassailable persona we project at work so no one can see how frightened we really are," Arthur stated in what I felt was a significant insight. "Sometimes I think we've both always been too afraid to see how much we've always needed our wives and others to support us."

As he began to see himself more clearly, Arthur was gradually able to recognize a more nuanced, complex portrait of his father, and in turn, to become much less critical of him. His need for his father to be so invincible in order for Arthur to defend against his own anxieties and limitations was lessening. He came to appreciate his father's capacity to reveal his more needy side because it not only validated Arthur's *own* vulnerabilities but also gave him permission to reveal these vulnerabilities. And in frequently visiting Everett during his recuperation, Arthur began to talk more openly about these feelings with his father.

As a result of Arthur's insights and changing attitudes, Everett felt more comfortable about the changes he was undergoing. It was evident from Arthur's account that both father and son were eschewing the rigid perception of masculinity they'd always clung to, as well as becoming more honest about when they were truly self-sufficient and when they needed help and support. This made it easier for Everett to accept his condition and find ways of living with it constructively. At the same time, Arthur was able to help Everett because he could finally accept the fact that his father needed help, just as he accepted his own need for my help, as his therapist.

MORE OPPORTUNITIES FOR MUTUAL GROWTH

Oftentimes the most significant change in the father-son relationship occurs when the son becomes a father himself. Although many older men look forward to becoming grandfathers, they soon find, in addition to pleasures both expected and unexpected, that they've entered a new developmental phase in which they become increasingly aware of their own aging and mortality. However, it's also the case, as the psychoanalyst Stanley Cath reminds us, that the actualities of becoming a grandfather serve to minimize some of the aging man's anxieties about his own impending death and frequently diminish existing problems with his children and heirs.[4]

Some older fathers and maturing sons find that their shared interaction with grandchildren allows them to address many of the thorny issues that previously divided them, even those that have passed from father to son. In this way, a grandchild's birth and consequent growth create opportunities for reworking the father-son relationship. For example, the son may resent his father's easy and grandfatherly acceptance of his grandson's interests and activities, the very ones he could not easily accept in his own son. The elder father may, at the same time, come to see his own son in a new way as he observes how he acclimates to his new parental responsibilities. For many men, grandfatherhood represents their last chance to create a tenderer, even "idealized" parental role, as this marks a chance to do it again the "right" way.

I recently consulted with an elderly father, Russell, and his thirty-five-year-old son, Eric. They came to work on some long-standing conflicts that continued to fester. Despite these issues, I recognized how deeply the two men were connected and how highly motivated each was to reconcile. After several sessions, they described an evening together in the preceding week when Eric made dinner at his home for his young son Mason and Russell. After dinner, nine-year-old Mason said he didn't want to clean the dishes as Eric had asked him to. "If I've told you once, I've told you a thousand times," Eric said, his loud voice filled with contempt, "you have responsibilities in this family but you are such a lazy kid and now you're in big trouble!"

No sooner were the words out of his mouth than he wished he could take them back. He knew that his tone was inappropriately harsh, and that Mason always reacted badly to his punitive voice. But what was worse was realizing in an instant that he had sounded just like his father. Russell had always spoken to him like that when he was a boy, and he'd hated it. That he recognized this— that he didn't shrink from seeing how identified he was with a loathed quality of his father's—was a mark of his own maturing adulthood. Men who can't face this kind of recognition, who insist on pretending that they are nothing like their fathers or have none of their fathers' undesirable traits, are then forced to conceal or deny these characteristics, often at great personal cost and harm to loved ones. Men like this tend to constrict themselves and frequently resort to blaming others for their own behaviors while continuing to evade responsibility for aspects of themselves that they would prefer not to acknowledge.

Mason had stomped out of the room when Russell said, "You're too hard on him, Eric. He's only nine." At these words, Eric felt himself grow furious. His father never had such compassion for him when *he* was nine years old; in fact, Russell had been an unusually strict and impatient father. Eric remembered how he'd hated all the responsibilities and restrictions he'd been forced to shoulder growing up. And here he was now, excusing his grandson for laziness, a trait he never tolerated in his own son!

In recounting his experience to both Russell and me, Eric noted that he took a moment to reflect before he said anything. Making full use of the insights he had acquired during our sessions, Eric realized that his father now had the opportunity to present his "best self" to his grandson precisely because he was *not* the boy's father. Russell wasn't responsible for Mason; he didn't need to enforce rules, instill moral values, or build his grandson's character. Released from these obligations, he was free to be more loving, indulgent, generous, tender, patient, and involved than he was as a father. Some grandfathers, Eric knew, took a very active role in grandparenting their grandchildren in an attempt to atone for their own shortcomings as fathers. Russell didn't feel the need to go to this extreme; but by defending his grandson, perhaps he was trying to make up for some of the mistakes he'd made when he was young.

Eric told Russell in our session that, for a few minutes after realizing this, he felt quite resentful, but soon these feelings transformed into empathy. Eric understood, for the first time, the frustration that his own father must have felt toward him when he was a child. Eric said to Russell: "Dad, I felt a wave of understanding that I'd never experienced before; suddenly I wished that I could apologize for all the times I'd hurt you." He added that now he knew how much these hurts could sting.

What happened to Eric, as Sam Osherson might explain, is that his "father wound"—the internalized, unresolved conflict between father and son that the son felt as an old and lasting internal injury—became activated by this interaction. Because Eric was now mature enough to constructively use our work together, he could start to take the necessary steps to repair the relationship and heal the wound. He could accomplish this by empathizing with his father rather than criticizing him and thereby distancing himself.

Russell also recognized this interaction with his son, and our processing of it, as significant. He mentioned that he'd never seen Eric be so angry or speak so harshly to Mason as he did that evening. He told Eric that he might have easily turned vindictive, saying something like: "So now you know what I went through. You see what it's like to have a son who doesn't respect you." But to his credit, Russell stopped himself. He told Eric that as a young father, he had more often than not treated him harshly. He always regretted that this was the case, but had come basically to accept it. He wasn't a perfect father, and neither was his son, but that needn't stop them from respecting each other now.

Russell and Eric were largely in agreement at this point that to be "good enough" is not to have done everything right, but rather, as I suggested in chapter 7, to admit to one's own limitations and failures in a way that frees one's son to pursue his own version of manhood. What made Russell and Eric especially lucky in this regard is that they had the opportunity to grow and deepen their understanding of their own experience side by side, in a shared interaction.

Russell was also very fortunate that Eric chose to include his father in his life. Many men struggle with feeling abandoned by their more fully differentiated sons. But the good enough father no longer requires that his adult son need or depend on him to confirm his own worth. The more the father accepts this, the more likely he is to help his son develop his own capacity to parent his own children, and to continue to grow as an adult as well. This letting go is a form of paternal altruism that reflects a father's mature empathy, whereby he is able to relinquish acting on his own needs for the sake of his son's further individuation. What is more, by accepting his son's more complete differentiation as a mature adult man, the older father is freer to pursue aspects of his own life that may have remained on hold during his own maturing years when he was concerned with establishing himself in the world and fathering in his own family.

This type of mutual help and recognition is possible without grandchildren to facilitate it. Having children is only the most literal expression of generativity. Men who don't become fathers themselves for various reasons still find ways to become generative. They can serve as mentors, coaches, and advisers in the workplace, or they can choose a helping profession such as social worker or educator. Indeed, this phase of life isn't necessarily about having biological children and grandchildren. Rather, it is about finding ways to give of oneself by nourishing those who are younger; and by relinquishing one's need to be in the limelight, to support the younger generation's ascension to center stage and their need to be autonomous.

A man in his later years is seeking to find meaning for his life and a sense of integrity during his old age. He comes to appreciate that he is what survives of him. In this respect, realistic immortality does *not* rest solely on biological or familial connections. In contrast, it resides in those actions and works that affect future generations through what a man constructs, imparts, and leaves behind in the people he has influenced and the creations he is responsible for. Erikson and his colleagues call this form of caring and nurturing in late life "grand-generativity."[5] It is evident not only in grandparenting, but in the mentoring that incorporates generational concern for the young of today in the future, for the young still unborn, and for the world's survival as a whole.

· · ·

RECONCILING DIFFERENCES

As sons and fathers mature together, their relationships, even their disagreements, begin to take on a different cast. They come to see that their differences are not necessarily threatening, dangerous, or evidence of someone being more powerful, but rather are topics and issues to talk about. As a result, their conversations, though often passionate, tend to be less hindered by anger, blaming, and defensiveness.

Blake, who was forty-one when he came to see me about his concern over his own son, was outgoing, social and personable. Bob, his sixty-nine-year-old father, was quiet, introspective, and shy. These differences caused them no end of conflict through the years. Bob had been very critical and disapproving when the teenage Blake was more interested in his social life than his grades; when Blake married at twenty-four; and later, when Blake and his wife separated for a while.

But now Blake was a middle-aged man, readily assuming responsibilities toward his children, his wife, and his career as a successful architect; and Bob was trying to come to terms with his retirement and his own aging. To their mutual surprise, over the last few years the two men found that they could discuss their differences in a new context. This seemed paradoxical because each was traveling in what appeared to be opposite directions—Blake struggling to let go of his boyishness so he could become more of a mature man; and Bob trying, for the first time in his life, to let go of his cautious "maturity" and become more spontaneous and playful. Blake mentioned that he saw himself and his father valuing the sides of one another that each had previously disdained. Moreover, Blake noted, both seemed to feel comfortable enough now to share confidences about their relationship.

In a recent exchange between them, Blake admitted that he always felt Bob viewed him as superficial and unintelligent; Bob confessed that he believed that Blake judged him uninteresting, boring, and dull. Never before had they been able to laugh about their past squabbles, and admit how much they envied one another's strengths while appreciating their differences. No one was a villain. They were just two mature men reaching a rapprochement through greater acceptance of themselves and their differences. Blake told me how important it was to him when his father had said, "I would have gone about my life differently than you, but then again, we are different men. I respect you and I am impressed how you are able to do things that I couldn't dream of."

However, the opportunity to further reconcile issues doesn't always occur so naturally in the course of a father and son's parallel maturation. Moreover, for many sons it can occur only in the *intrapsychic realm*—that is, only within themselves, in their minds and hearts—because their fathers are either unavailable or dead. This requires the son to mourn for the idealized father he had always wanted, and in turn, come to better understand and appreciate the father he had.

For instance, Arnie, a forty-one-year-old father of two young children, was somewhat depressed when he began therapy with me. His relationship with his rather distant father during the course of Arnie's childhood was marked by sadness and loss. He reported early in his therapy how he often dreamt of his deceased father, Sam, a hardworking but taciturn butcher in Boston. Because Sam was typically too tired or involved in his business to be much of a presence at home, Sam's wife essentially ran the family. Arnie often complained about his father's lack of involvement, lamenting his absence. The only time he stopped complaining was when he recalled brief but meaningful chats about their beloved Boston Red Sox.

During one session, Arnie told me that he'd dreamt about his son's recent bar mitzvah, and the pleasure he'd felt in seeing his own son wearing Sam's prayer shawl. Arnie then remembered looking out into the congregation and feeling shocked to see his father, Sam, wearing a Red Sox cap instead of a yarmulke, sitting proudly among the guests gathered for the event. He saw Sam admiring his grandson in a way Arnie felt he had never admired him. He awoke from the dream feeling confused but strangely calm.

As Arnie and I began to sort out the dream's meaning together, he realized that he wished his father could have gotten to know his grandson and be a part of his life (Sam died when the boy was just two years old). For the first time, Arnie began to grieve more fully for his own "lost" father. After that session, the tenor of our discussions began to change. Over the next few months, Arnie thought less and less about what he had always wanted more of, and instead started focusing on what he would have liked to have understood about his father or might have been able to give him if he were alive. Though Arnie didn't realize it at the time, he was in the midst of reconciling with his dead father, a process that reached its culmination several years later when the Red Sox won the 2004 World Series. Shortly thereafter, Arnie went to the cemetery for the first time since the year after Sam had died. He placed a brand-new Red Sox cap on his father's grave—a fitting tribute and farewell to his father, and a touching acknowledgment that his indictments were now obsolete.

COPING WITH LOSS

Despite all the rewards inherent in the father-son relationship when it enters this stage, the reality is that both men have to contend with issues of loss in relation to each other. Mature, adult-aged sons have to face the fact that their fathers are no longer so strong and powerful, while aging fathers must confront the loss of their young sons.

By acknowledging his son's adulthood, a father begins to experience a psychological "empty nest." As long as their younger sons were primarily engaged in trying to find their way in the world, fathers could still feel useful and important as protectors and guides. Now that the sons have differentiated themselves, by creating their own families and establishing themselves in their work and professional lives, fathers often feel diminished.

Mothers typically go through this "empty nest" phenomenon before fathers do. At each of the previous major individuations— during toddlerhood, adolescence, and young adulthood—sons separate from their mothers and turn to their fathers for guidance, leaving their mothers bereft while the fathers, by identifying with their sons during these individuations, have the opportunity to enjoy a newfound closeness. Eventually, however, as the sons become mature adults with families themselves, these feelings of loss catch up with fathers, who find themselves out of a job along with their wives.

Many older men struggle with being displaced by sons who are not only their equal but surpass them in many respects. As an aging father experiences his own physical decline, he may become critical of his son in an attempt to regain the control he feels himself losing; other fathers may withdraw completely. An aging father who is psychologically mature will find ways to bear and contain his difficult feelings of loss, exclusion, and envy. This father will not work against his maturing son's individuation but will rather support it. This commonly calls for the father to find new avenues to confirm his sense of worthiness, no longer requiring his son's need for him to bolster his own self-esteem. In fact, when a father is able to recognize that the younger man is now his equal while minimally dependent on him, it signals his own success as a father.

For their part, sons begin to realize that their fathers can no longer protect them or offer security. This is the realization that Simon faced when his infant son became critically ill. An even starker recognition awaits, however, as the developmental psychiatrist Roger Gould reminds us: most men in their thirties acknowledge the fading away of an illusion that has helped them arrive at adulthood, namely, "the illusion of absolute safety."[6] Not only can fathers not protect them, but there is ultimately no protection at all.

Essentially, both father and son are now facing their own existential vulnerability, the vagaries and uncertainties of life itself. That which offered them safety—work, achievement, material possessions, family, and friendship—is revealed as transitory. It is not that these qualities aren't significant, but rather that they offer no security against aging, infirmity, and death. Coming to terms with one's mortality is the central issue at midlife and will serve as a major point of connection for the maturing son and his elderly father for the remainder of their lives. The inevitability of death leads inexorably to another vital realization, namely, that life is precious and that we all have a responsibility to make each moment meaningful. There's nothing worse, to the maturing man, than "time wasted." It's no surprise that such great philosophers as Camus, Sartre, Kierkegaard, and Kafka, who identified and illuminated the "existential crisis," accomplished their groundbreaking work when they themselves were at this critical phase of development.

The maturing adult son and his aging father are on a parallel course where lost illusions must be mourned and the limitations of one's self, loved ones, and reality accepted. Each man can benefit from the other's experience and wisdom as they confront these issues. At times, a father can help his son face these challenges, and there will be opportunities for a mature son to serve his father in similar fashion. When father and son are able to share their understanding of the fleeting nature of time, they provide recognition to one another and solace in authentically facing life's uncertainties.

This man-to-man dialogue takes on new meaning at this stage. Some years ago, I recall overhearing a conversation between my neighbor, Mitch, and his father, Alfred, in Mitch's backyard over a barbecue. Mitch said to his father, "You know, when I was a teenager, I remember thinking to myself that you didn't know anything. Now, I look back and suppose that the older I get, the smarter you become."

Alfred laughed. "I remember thinking the same thing about my father." Mitch smiled ruefully, then said, "I thought that once I'd come this far in life"—he indicated his large Spanish-style home, his sizable backyard, the swing set for the kids—"I'd have no more worries."

"There are always worries," Alfred said. Mitch seemed to want to take the conversation deeper, perhaps to discover how his father felt about his station in life.

"Is this all there is?" Mitch asked.

"I know what you're asking and I wish I knew, son," Alfred replied. Although Mitch felt a little shaken by his father's uncertainty, he also felt relieved. When he noticed that I'd overheard their conversation, Mitch told me that at least he and his father were finally in the same boat to converse about these issues. Now that they'd broached the subject, Mitch looked forward to many more conversations.

• • •

THE TRANSITION INTO MIDLIFE

For all these reconciliations and profound insights, maturing adulthood is often seen as a rich time of life, full of unexpected challenges and rewards. It culminates in the so-called "midlife transition" which, if not tackled adequately, often serves as the precursor to what is commonly known as the "midlife crisis," the signs of which—the new red sports car in the driveway; a divorce followed by a younger trophy wife; a reckless outdoor escapade resulting in physical injuries—have become a cultural cliché.

But a man's midlife challenge is far from a joke. Nothing is more real than discovering, once and for all, that one is no longer "young," and that it's time to address the fundamental questions about one's life's purpose. At midlife a man also begins to experience an urgency to act as he becomes increasingly aware of the limits of time.

It is at midlife that we first deal with the loss of youth, try to match the percept of an aging self with the memory of a younger self, begin to perceive the passage of time differently, and relate more personally to death, with an accompanying realization of the finite amount of time left. For most men, by the age of forty-five, the *biological* decline is unmistakable; death is no longer an abstract possibility, but a relatively steady companion conveying one's inescapable fate. A sense of urgency, reaching a plateau in the workplace, and reversing roles with respect to aging parents typically come to mark middle age. The young man's efforts to prove his manliness begin to attenuate, the adaptive grandiosity of early adulthood lessens, and one's shortcomings are quite evident.

The midlife transition—signaled by the confrontation with

one's personal death and its attendant anxieties—optimally leads to further transformations of the male ego, especially in the decline of phallic masculinity. A new set of tasks appears, pertaining less to establishing one's *sense of identity* in the world and more to the *need for meaning*. Parts of the psyche that were necessarily renounced or repudiated previously in order to establish a stable sense of identity are awakened during life's second half. Priority is given to insight, connection, and nurturance—unless a more pathological upsurge of defensive phallicism occurs, in which case gender polarity is further strengthened and becomes a powerful obstacle to midlife development.

Men during this period experience considerable inner turmoil associated with the renunciation of illusions and the acceptance of their limitations. The man at midlife often experiences a sense of ennui and a "depressive crisis" that reflects the pain inherent in having had to restrict oneself psychically in order to achieve sufficient mastery in the arena of external action. This constriction of the self produces a developmental need both to reclaim those parts of the self that may have been disavowed earlier in life in order to achieve a more socially acceptable sense of masculinity, and to come to terms with one's limitations. Such a psychological task then requires each individual to shift to a more inward, integrative perspective, embracing the lost parts of the self.[7]

Typically, a man enters his transition phase sometime between the ages of forty and forty-five. These years work as a bridge from maturing adulthood to middle and late adulthood; and to weather this transitional period successfully, there are three main tasks. First, men are called upon to review and reappraise their lives to date. Next, they must modify their lives, taking the first steps toward entering middle adulthood, making choices, and testing out new hypotheses. Finally, they have to set the course on which they will ultimately resolve the critical polarities of midlife that are the sources of deep division in their inner lives.[8]

For the majority of men, this stage of development evokes tumultuous struggle both within the self and externally. Every aspect of a man's life comes into question, and it is often terrifying for a man to face what is being revealed to him about himself. He entertains confusion, doubt, emotional turmoil, despair, and feelings of immobility; in this sense, this period is much like that of adolescence. And just as they did when they were teenagers, men benefit from having a strong relationship with their fathers, or their internalized fathers if the older men have died, as the following vignette illustrates.

Stanley, the forty-three-year-old father of a young boy, had built up a successful career that left him financially independent and contributed to his strong sense of masculinity. Working hard also helped him to ward off the depressive anxiety to which he'd always been prone. However, over the past year, he'd no longer felt as driven to develop his business further, which perplexed him. He began feeling increasingly unhappy. After undergoing major knee surgery, he was distressed that his body was "starting to fail." In addition, his son was more interested in drawing and going to museums than in sports, and his wife was becoming moody and volatile.

When Stanley first showed up at my office, he told me that he wanted me to help him figure out what he might do to help his wife be less irritable, depressed, and angry. Yet, after a few sessions, he admitted that he himself felt as if he were entering a dark, ominous "valley of the unknown," which threatened to engulf him.

Stanley was the only son of an aloof yet distinguished professor and his much younger immigrant wife. His already elderly father died when Stanley was just eight years old. Stanley became tearful as he talked about his father, though he hastened to add that he "took after" the older man in terms of being similarly aloof. Although he'd remained very close with his mother despite her "flakiness," he now felt inexplicably abandoned and ashamed.

"I don't know what I'm supposed to do and what's supposed to happen next," he complained soon after beginning his psychoanalysis. Dismayed by our apparent lack of progress, he wished our work was more like "surgery, where I can just trust my doctor to put me to sleep and correct whatever damage may be in my body." In distinction to the powerful surgeon, or father, who could render him unconscious and repair the damage, I initially represented a more powerless motherlike figure, who stood for such nebulous things as "relationship" and "emotions" rather than the more highly valued paternal qualities of "discovery" and "knowledge."

Stanley's confusion gradually gave way to anger with the therapeutic process, and considerable impatience with me. He took the position he imagined his father would have taken, that of a "skeptic" who would tease and oppose his mother's "unscientific" forays into the less material, "touchy-feely" realms. Stanley couldn't understand, for example, why I was interested in exploring his relationship with his parents, because that wasn't the "real" problem. He repeatedly insisted that he'd come to therapy in order to find a way of altering his wife's behavior toward him, or at least to find a better way to live with her. "What's the point of all this emotion and how will it improve my marriage?" he demanded. To me, Stanley was expressing his fear of being left alone in the seemingly illogical, "feminine" terrain of feelings that he associated with his mother.

Not surprisingly, whenever Stanley made any emotional contact with himself, he would quickly crush it by becoming detached and overly intellectualized. I interpreted to him that he would abruptly disappear from his "feeling" self in a way that was similar to how he might have experienced his father's sudden death. That is, without his father to help support his masculinity, he drew very clear boundaries around what he defined as masculine behavior. These would protect him from his fear of being drawn into the more "flaky," feminine, chaotic interior world he associated with his wife and mother, and now with me. I proposed that he didn't want to show me how "thirsty" he was for his father because to do so would revive both his feelings of fatherly loss and his deep needs for his mother's comfort. He recognized how often he felt ashamed to expose these basic feelings because he "might be seen as defective."

In what psychoanalysts refer to as "the transference," Stanley harbored feelings toward me that he'd had toward his own father.[9] He needed me to become his surrogate father, someone who could help Stanley access his lost father inside himself. As Stanley came to respect and feel safe with me—and to trust that I understood him—he was gradually more able to experience me as a man who could contain his own chaotic and fearful internal world while staying psychologically close to him. In turn, he could mourn both the loss of his actual father and the parts of himself he'd had to repudiate in an effort to erect a stable but unnecessarily rigid sense of masculinity.

Stanley's midlife transition became an anxious, shame-dominated "midlife crisis" because he couldn't reconcile his new definition of what it meant to be a man with the notion of masculinity that he'd developed years ago. He desperately needed both to reclaim the lost parts of his self and to come to terms with his limitations. Fortunately for him, our work together helped him achieve a more nuanced, comprehensive sense of masculinity. He no longer needed to eschew his interior world of feeling, need, and

intense longing in order to feel appreciated by a male presence.
As a result, the less worried he became about "being a man," the
more he was able to experience a healthier relationship with both
his wife and son.

Once the midlife transition has been accomplished, many men
find themselves entering into the new domains of middle and late
adulthood, a time during which they tend to turn inward and
place less emphasis on the assertiveness and mastery of the environment that had been so important during the formative adult
stages. Bernice Neugarten, a developmental psychologist, identifies this basic midlife change as an "increased interiority of the
personality."[10] Instead of trying to attain specific goals, the man
at midlife is oriented toward realizing a greater enjoyment of the
process of living.

Yet this is also a time when men realize that, in addition to
fathering their own children, they are becoming increasing
responsible for their aging fathers. A reversal of the generations
is well underway, and the death of one's father, if it hasn't already
occurred, will soon come to pass. A sense of impending mortality colors the years ahead, including the emotional landscape
through which fathers and sons travel together. The middle-aged
son, now a senior or "elder" man in his own right, must carry on
the paternal imprimatur for future generations.

9

REVERSING ROLES IN LATER LIFE

*I am of old and young, of the foolish as much as
the wise,
Regardless of others, ever regardful of others,
Maternal as well as paternal, a child, as well as
a man . . .*

—WALT WHITMAN[1]

It is not uncommon for middle-aged men and their elderly
fathers to find their relationship taking a difficult, oftentimes
awkward turn. After years of stability and equality, the scales
have tipped as older men increasingly depend on their sons for
physical, emotional, and at times financial support. This reality—that sons ultimately end up parenting their own fathers
often at the same time that they are still parenting their children—can cause great anguish for both father and son.

Yet, ironically, this is also a time during which both men find themselves closer than they've been in years. Facing their mortality, feeling the urgent need to make good use of the time left to them, father and son are ready to give up past illusions and come to grips with what's real and important in their lives. They find themselves coping with similar changes and, as a result, they arrive at comparable realizations, such as the shared understanding of how important it is to remain generative and helpful to others, and to find constructive ways of grappling with their complex feelings about one another and possible despair over aging. Because of this congruence, they are particularly well suited to share with and support one another, as well as to forge new and deeper connections.

MIDLIFE AND TURNING INWARD

Men in their late forties, fifties, and sixties, entering the fourth individuation, are coming to terms with their own physical and emotional limitations as well as the death of their heroic aspirations. During middle age and later life, men experience a developmental need to reclaim those less action-oriented, receptive parts of themselves that were necessarily constricted for them to achieve sufficient mastery in the world and accommodate to society's ideal of manhood. Now they need to reconfigure the boyish, ever youthful parts of themselves so that they can successfully face the aging process in their years ahead.[2]

During midlife, the very nature of a man's quest changes. Until this point he has focused almost exclusively on establishing his *identity* to serve him in the world at large and internally, as a man. However, now he is motivated by the need to find a *sense of meaning*, to settle on a new purpose that will influence the remaining years of his life and work. He needs to dismantle the framework that previously existed and replace it with something more durable, yet flexible enough to adapt to the imminent challenges ahead.

As a result of the biological and psychological changes occurring during this time, many men no longer are driven to prove their manhood but instead are freer to more fully be themselves. The male ego typically becomes less sharply gendered as the older man shifts from his action-oriented modes of being to a more inward, integrative perspective where the lost or scorned parts of his self can be embraced. Many men at this time attempt to resolve the tendency to see the world in terms of the basic polarities that have been a source of division in their life—young versus old, masculine versus feminine, active versus passive, good versus evil, alone versus attached—and begin to understand that answers lie not in either/or choices but rather somewhere along the continuum, seeking a balance among these polar extremes.

In the second half of life, most men naturally begin to turn inward as their sense of certainty is being dismantled. Rather than pursuing specific goals and trying to master his environment—important goals throughout his formative years—the man at midlife is increasingly oriented toward enjoying the process of living. This inward journey often involves acknowledging mistakes and weaknesses, as well as revealing secrets. In particular, a man is faced with the need to acknowledge and accept his own limitations, above all as a father, in order to move into the final phase of his life with a realistic yet hopeful attitude. In short, he's faced with what I've described as the "necessity of growing small in order to become whole."[3] With the waning of the "heroic" version of himself that he created to succeed in the world of younger adults, a man's experience of himself as the center of his heroic journey is coming to an end. When he can accomplish these tasks of life's second half, he is less likely to view his life with a sense of despair or defeat. Instead, he remains accepting and hopeful, eager to find new ways to become generative and creative.

This isn't an easy task. Some men find it mortifying to recognize their limitations and come to terms with their failures in their parental roles, consequently leaving their sons a legacy of unresolved grief, guilt, and bitter remorse. Mel Lansky, a psychoanalyst and family therapist, offers a richly textured portrait of fathers who fail.[4] Though he studied middle-aged fathers, largely those between thirty-five to fifty-five years old who were hospitalized in a family treatment program, his findings are relevant to all aging men and their fathers. In particular, he found that men often go to extraordinary lengths to avoid the shame and humiliation of confronting their inability to "father" their own children. The emotional vulnerability and shame associated with being an inadequate father are often unbearable for many men. Thus, they do whatever they can—blaming others, impulsively acting out, and obsessively focusing on distractions in order to avoid facing up to their shortcomings as fathers and experiencing their own pain.

Those elderly fathers who can find ways to overcome their shame help not only themselves but their sons as well. James, a patient of mine in his late forties, had as a child always resented his father Roy for his emotional and oftentimes physical absence from the life of his family. Nonetheless, James's resentment remained buried throughout most of his childhood, and even now as an adult, his relationship with his father was politely constrained. James and Roy never argued or fought as each man seemed to go his own way rather than risk conflict or genuine closeness. In discussing how this cordiality masked the distance between them, James told me that he felt responsible because he "never really opened up" to his father, whom he "never forgave." Though they saw one another fairly frequently, the distance between himself and his father seemed to James like "a Grand Canyon."

However, all of this changed quite unexpectedly late in our first year of working together when Roy, now in his mid-seventies, suffered a life-threatening aneurism. During his recovery, James frequently visited Roy at the hospital and told me how surprised he was during one visit to find his father musing freely about his own father. James went on to tell me how shocked he was when his father became tearful in telling him that his father, "Grandpa Joe," had a serious heart condition his whole life and that it took a big toll on Roy and his sisters. Roy added: "We always had to tiptoe around him, not to get him upset, and I realize that I was that kind of father to you. My dad couldn't be more active in our lives, but I could have; only I chose not to and I feel badly about it. I just didn't know how to do it any differently, but I wish I had."

Although James knew that Roy had had a distant relationship with his father, he had never known about his grandfather's condition, nor how much Roy had suffered as a result. Until that moment of facing his own mortality, Roy hadn't felt comfortable disclosing his unrelenting childhood pain and the ways in which he was hurt by his father. Nor had Roy ever let on that he himself felt badly about his own fathering. As James and I discussed the impact of his father's disclosures, it was evident that he welcomed the information and especially Roy's unexpected willingness to be vulnerable with him.

During the next several sessions, James began to view his father's behavior in a historical context. "My God," he told me, "Dad must have been terrified about possibly upsetting Grandpa, fearful about expressing his feelings, so no wonder he's always seemed so cut off and far away." James realized that his father carried a deep sense that his feelings, particularly negative ones, could "kill" loved ones, and consequently, he needed to withdraw largely to preserve and protect. He began to understand that unconsciously, he was following this familial code where it seemed better to close down than risk upsetting someone that you care about. With this insight, James no longer worried that he hadn't been a respectable son, nor did he need to take his father's emotional absence so personally. In brief, because Roy finally felt safe enough to reveal his own pain and guilt to his son, James was able to use our work together to help him begin to forgive Roy for his absence from his life. James also found himself more readily accepting his own shortcomings as a man and father.

FATHERS OFFER A MODEL FOR GROWING OLD

Fathers also help their sons navigate middle age by accepting their own aging. Our culture is full of pejorative stereotypes when it comes to growing old; just think of the negative colloquialisms we use to describe it, in phrases like "put out to pasture" and "fading fast." Despite the idealized images of white-haired elders we see in commercials, our culture celebrates youth and disparages aging. We view it as defeat, as undignified, disgusting, and shameful.

A father who fights these stereotypes, who has made peace with his age, and who isn't preoccupied with youth but rather finds ways to remain physically, sexually, emotionally, and mentally active and vital, will serve as a good model for his middle-aged son. Such modeling continues as fathers cope with the challenges of illness, senescence, and death, which mark the fifth individuation, typically beginning during his late sixties and beyond. This penultimate individuation process precedes death, which may be considered the final individuation. Involving the aging man's ongoing separations from aspects of his own, earlier self, it occurs when, at the end of his life, he comes to truly appreciate that he is, in essence, what survives him. In meeting this challenge, the elderly father accepts the nearness of death and prepares for it.

The aged father must take stock of a profound intrapsychic change in which he is shifting from being the one *who is left* to the one *who is leaving*. At the same time, stimulated by his acceptance of his impending personal end, he feels a strong desire to give generously of his wisdom and possessions. In this way, an elderly father becomes like Hermes of Greek mythology, the god who guides souls to the underworld. Descending toward death, the father eases his son's passage into later adulthood by accepting in himself the need to go downward or inward in order to find "the light," and to come to terms with his own inevitable mortality. Furthermore, by renouncing any illusions of living forever, the father, in his final mentoring function, can show his son how to die wisely.

In an ideal situation, a father models what the psychoanalyst Cal Colarusso calls "genetic immortality" for his son.[5] By remaining personally active and involved in his son's life, recognizing his son's otherness, and maintaining an affectionate but well-differentiated relationship with him, the elderly father comes to trust that his provisions for his son have been worthwhile. Moreover, the father has come to believe that his son's existence has ultimately become more important than his own life, and in this way, the elderly father sets the stage for fostering his son's continuing

growth and development. Such a realization often makes it easier for these men to accept their own demise, which, in turn,
will ease their son's grief and help the younger man to approach
the reality of his own death with more equanimity when the
time comes.

As I noted in chapter 8, this ability to become concerned
about those who will live in the more distant future is known as
"grand-generativity." Just as grandparents are more concerned
with their grandchildren's general development than their day-
to-day lives, so "grand-generativity" refers to a generational concern for youth and subsequent generations to come, for those
not yet born, and for the world at large. Men who feel pleasure
in the pleasures of others, are concerned about events not
directly related to their own self-interest, and are able to invest
themselves in tomorrow's world, are more likely to leave a
legacy that their sons and grandsons can benefit directly from.
This capacity for ego transcendence rather than ego preoccupation in late life, as Bernice Neugarten and her research collabo-
rators observed, enables the elderly man to experience the
pleasures of the moment, enjoy his old age, and thereby age more
gracefully.[6] Moreover, the older father who experiences this generational concern is able to achieve a sense of *realistic immortality*, both for himself and for his middle-aged son.

Not all fathers, however, are able to model such successful
aging for their sons. Some resent the fact that power has shifted,
that they suddenly find themselves dependent and in need of
medical, emotional, and even financial support from their children for the first time. Others find themselves swamped with
envious, even destructive wishes toward their sons, who they see
as being healthier and younger, and therefore more powerful.
When such negative feelings cannot be contained, these fathers
often turn critical and rejecting of their sons.

In contrast, some fathers poignantly struggle with the fact that they are viewing their son's decline for the first time. For all the preceding years, the father has watched his son ascend to full manhood—at work, at home, in his community—and identified with him. But now, for the first time, the middle-aged son is himself descending into late adulthood and is no longer a "young hero." Some fathers may handle this type of disillusionment by becoming critical of their sons' ability to take care of themselves, in effect, angrily displacing their own worries about aging and being dependent onto their sons. Instead of lashing out toward his son, however, an older father needs to find new ways to accommodate to his own situation and further ways to grow. He may no longer be able to satisfy his own heroic ideal through his son's journey. Instead, in respecting his son's unique middle-life experiences, he has to confront his own aging and decline directly, and by doing so, discover how he can experience the integrity of his own life.

SONS HELPING FATHERS

Besides helping their sons negotiate middle age, elderly fathers have their own challenges to face. During late adulthood, certain preoccupations about time passing and personal death that first took root during middle adulthood intensify and become more compelling. In addition, a father must struggle with his own complex feelings about his son (and other children), as well as his reaction to their likely ambivalences toward him.

Erikson describes this stage of life as a time when men experience the conflict between the sense of integrity and that of disgust and despair.[7] Thus, an elderly man attempts, at this point, to balance his anxieties and desolation with the knowledge that his life was, in fact, an achievement that he can think of with gratitude and pride. The fortunate man feels satisfied that his life was, as a whole, meaningful and of value. He attempts to live in the present, to stay active and engaged despite physical and emotional limitations, negotiating between feeling depleted and feeling restored.

For their part, middle-aged sons become more accepting of their own limitations and increasingly aware of the limits of time. They find themselves better able to let go of past resentments and discover ways to accept the love their fathers offered them, however imperfect it may have been. Even men whose relationships with their fathers had been highly troubled often feel the need to reestablish ties with their aging father before death renders such physical reconciliation impossible. At the same time, for the father who has not been very successful in his fathering, it may not be too late to accomplish some reparation that can contribute to both son and father. In short, during their mid- and later lives, fathers and sons are intrinsically drawn toward forgiveness and reconciliation—and not just those who are in therapy. I believe that there is an innate, albeit unconscious motivation to make amends, and hopefully they will each have opportunities to do so.

Allen, a patient of mine in his late fifties, recently told me about a visit he had with Ned, his eighty-six-year-old father, who now lives in a retirement community in Arizona. For years, Allen complained about his father's unquenchable and seemingly limitless narcissism, how the older man was never able to focus on his son but appeared to care only about himself. Allen had been working hard in his therapy to understand himself better, and in doing so, he began to look more deeply into his father's history and, as a result, appreciate who his father was. Ned was the only child of Scandinavian immigrant parents, who worked long days in menial jobs and drank themselves to sleep in the evening. In realizing that Ned "never really had a father who was there for him," Allen began to empathize with Ned's bitterness and inner emptiness. Though still finding it difficult to spend much time with his father, Allen's anger was lessening and becoming replaced by compassion for his father's plight. He was realizing that Ned simply couldn't give him what he didn't have inside to give. Over the course of many months, Allen understood that although Ned couldn't provide the kind of fathering he had always wished for, he could nonetheless find ways of seeing Ned's efforts to express his love and concern in his more limited fashion. Allen felt good about understanding that he was no longer so helpless either to receive from or give back to his father.

During Allen's most recent visit, Ned spent hours going through scrapbooks he'd insisted that his wife compile detailing all of his professional and athletic triumphs. "For the first time," Allen told me, "watching him turn the pages of that book with his hands all blotchy and trembling, I realized that this was his way of trying to reach out to me. That in a way, my father was offering himself to me. He was trying to say, 'I wanted to be good, so I could be good for you.' I never thought of it that way; I'd only heard him as bragging about his achievements. But now, trying to push my own resentments aside as I watched this sad old man try to reach out to me, I understood that he was trying to prove himself worthy enough of me so that I'd think well of him. He couldn't do it any other way. Suddenly I realized that there was no point in wishing he'd been otherwise—he was imperfect, and I was, too. I'd never felt so tenderly toward him in my life."

Ned experienced his son's appreciation. As a result, he relaxed some and both men became more comfortable in being together. Ned sensed that he didn't have to keep proving he was a good father and successful man; furthermore, no longer so driven to justify himself, he could feel proud of Allen and express this directly to him. Though Ned still had a long road to travel before he could attain a more stable sense of integrity in later life, he'd taken a huge step forward thanks largely to Allen, whose insight and forgiveness helped ensure that the end of his father's life was weighted toward meaning and continuity rather than isolation, despair, and bitterness.

Isolation and loneliness are certainly pressing problems for the elderly. As their spouses, relatives, and friends grow ill and die, older fathers feel increasingly alone. Because men tend to die at a younger age than women, the men who do survive tend to have fewer same-sex companions to share their later lives with. Moreover, because women often surround them, older men find themselves especially hungry for male companionship. A son who steps in as a friend and confidant can provide connection and intimacy that are both meaningful and rejuvenating. Indeed, being close to another person in later life helps to prevent more disabling forms of loneliness and despair. As the geriatric researcher and psychiatrist Ewald Busse found, having a confidant is the most significant factor in differentiating elderly persons who were institutionalized from those who could actively remain in the community.[8]

By becoming more of a presence in his father's life, a middle-aged son can aid his father to maintain his interests, focus on others, and remain socially engaged. This is not always easy, there are often obstacles and setbacks, but a determined son can find ways to keep his father active in life.

I was lucky enough to be able to play such a role with my own father. Late in his life, he became quite ill and feeble, but throughout everything he retained his love for sports, particularly baseball. Because this was a love he'd shared with me, we always had plenty to talk about as we watched games together during my visits with him at his retirement home. During one of those visits, I realized that I wanted to take him to a game. Though he was somewhat confused, suffered from memory loss, and had difficulty walking, I had a feeling that he'd love a day at the ballpark. A week later, I drove him—and his walker—to Dodger Stadium, where we could watch our beloved Dodgers play. The logistics weren't easy; we each had to bear considerable physical discomfort and there was enough impatience and embarrassment on both sides to go around. But we pulled it off together, and in the end, the afternoon had enriched each of us in ways we both could immediately acknowledge.

For months, whenever I came to visit him, and even years later in his nursing home, I'd mention our afternoon. On the days when he could remember it, the memory never failed to bring a knowing smile to his face. As for me, I reaped a triple pleasure: that I was able to make it happen; that my father accepted the gift of the afternoon so graciously; and that I could partially reciprocate for all those games that he had taken me to as a youngster.

Not all fathers can accept such gifts from their sons, however. Some men can't get past the embarrassment, anger, and fear of having to turn to a son for help, whether financial, emotional, or physical. As a result, the older man sometimes acts out by rejecting or criticizing his son, or by attempting to keep the son in his place, all of which ultimately prove to be destructive and self-defeating in the long run.

Warren, for example, was a middle-aged man who sought my help for a reactive depression following his father's death. Warren had always tried to be an understanding son to his father, Charles. In describing the situation to me, this seemed especially true after Warren's mother died and he became instrumental in helping Charles sell his house and move into a retirement home.

According to Charles, however, Warren never did enough for him. The more he criticized Warren for not being a better son, the more resentful both of them became; naturally, this caused further strain between them and Warren chose to visit his father less frequently. As a result, Charles felt increasingly isolated in his attempt to prove that no one was good enough to care for him the way he needed to be cared for. Warren knew that he had to protect himself from his father's attacks, yet he felt tremendous guilt for not visiting as often as he thought he should.

Their labored relationship became an endurance match and both men suffered immeasurably. Eventually, several years later, Charles died as he had lived: isolated, despairing, and bitterly blaming others for his misfortune. Though Warren experienced a superficial relief that "I won't have to feel so guilty about not wanting to spend more time with him now," he was still at war with himself since, on a deeper level, nothing had been resolved with his father. He kept wishing he'd been able to say the magic word so that Charles would have treated him with more kindness and understanding; at the same time, he was plagued with guilt for wishing that his father had died more quickly. Consumed by unresolved grief, he was unable to move ahead or to mourn his father's death.

Eventually, Warren's self-denigration and despair led him into treatment, where I sought to help him attain a better understanding of the basis for his melancholic reaction to his father's death. In exploring his intensely conflicted feelings and needs in relation to Charles, particularly the more unacceptable ones, his depression began to lift. Warren eventually realized that the problem wasn't that he didn't offer enough help, but that his father never learned how to accept it. With this insight, Warren could finally feel his sadness and begin to grieve for himself and for the father he so desperately longed for.

I surmised that Charles's late-life difficulties reflected his struggle to both give and take. He had been an isolated man most of his life, who had never bonded well with his son, for which both father and son paid a steep price, especially during Charles's demise. In distinction to Charles, however, most fathers—particularly those who continue to remain involved with their sons— are better able to overcome their late-life struggle with their own limitations and can consequently appreciate the care given to them by their sons. These good enough fathers manage to see past their own anger and frustration over aging and their dependency, and to understand that their sons can offer help to them now primarily because they were raised well. In a sense, they are reaping the fruits of their own generativity.

A sensitive son may need to realize that his father's battles are really internal, that perhaps his aging father is fighting his own self. Appearing weak, passive, and even helpless in relation to another man, particularly his son, can be painful and distressing for the father. In addition, it can also impact his son detrimentally if his father acts out those feelings by rejecting the son or becoming critical, as Charles did. Ideally, a son needs to find ways to defuse the power struggle and offer help in a fashion that doesn't demean the older man—ways that encourage his father to feel necessary instead of superfluous. A son's recognition of his father's vulnerabilities can go a long way toward this end.

Ernie, for example, the patient of a therapist whom I supervised, was the owner of a plant nursery. His father, Gene, once a financial wizard, had made a fortune in the stock market. In fact, Gene had lent Ernie the money to begin his business. For years, Ernie relied on his father for investment advice; but after Gene suffered a stroke, he was no longer able to keep track of his investments. It was Ernie's turn to take over, a fact that made his father very nervous. Gene's masculinity, like so many men's, was directly linked to his sense of potency in the world and to his feeling neither dependent on others nor depleted within. At first, Gene demanded that Ernie show him every transaction. Ernie realized what was at stake, and made sure to ask his father for advice and to include his dad in all the decisions he made. As Gene saw that Ernie still valued his opinion, the older man congratulated himself on raising such a fine and intelligent son, which in turn helped him to relax and to give up more control.

Ernie's sensitivity to his father's feelings of loss and dependency helped Gene recognize and accept his own limitations. To his credit, according to my supervisee's reporting of Ernie's observations, Gene was then able to transform his view of himself as someone who could still be valued even though he wasn't in charge. He was beginning to overcome his need to *always* be the stronger, more independent one, and as a result, was learning to accept and express pleasure in his son's ability to give of himself. Most significantly, he was beginning to find meaning in opening up to the less developed sides of himself that he previously scorned as unmanly.

Like most men in later life, Gene sought to find meaning and self-acceptance. As I noted at the beginning of this chapter, aging men often focus on resolution, both within the sphere of relationships with others and in terms of the contradictions within themselves. Even those who ascribe to the more stereotypically "male" code of being dominant and independent, as Gene presumably had, tend to become more affiliative, nurturing, receptive, and less aggressive. In essence, most aging men are increasingly able to access and use parts of themselves that they may have previously regarded as feminine, such as becoming more expressive and committed to relationships. A man in his later years, as cross-cultural psychologist David Gutmann reports from observations across a variety of cultures, becomes more androgynous.[9]

However, as my own research has demonstrated, this expansion in an aging man's gendered sense of self, in contrast to his earlier years, does not necessarily diminish his feelings of being male. In fact, for most mature men, their sense of masculinity becomes at once more fluid and yet complex.

GRIEVING A FATHER'S DEATH

Elderly fathers approaching death often contemplate the legacies they will leave behind. Those fathers who can look back at the end of their lives and realize how they have helped their sons to master the physical, mental, and emotional hurdles along the way attain a deeper sense of self-worth while fulfilling their wishes for continuity. This lifelong masculine alliance between a father and his son is the culmination of what the Finnish psychoanalyst Vesa Manninen calls the "inevitable male project." Through their reciprocal, active engagement, fathers know that they will achieve immortality by living on in their sons' hearts and minds. As Manninen explains:

> If the father can trust that his offering to his son has been worthwhile and that he lives in his son's mind without forcing him to dependency, and that he thus is now and forever a blessing part of the son's independent growth, his own perishability will turn naturally to the reaching of eternity.[10]

A father who knows that his son has been able to learn from him in this way can perhaps bear the most difficult challenge of his existence: the overcoming of death itself. For sons, the process of bidding a father farewell is more complicated and protracted than merely attending a memorial service or throwing dirt on a grave. According to an old Gypsy proverb, "You have to dig deep to bury your father." In other words, as many sons discover, a great deal of work needs to be done after a father's death, including realizing the ways fathers remain alive inside them. By undertaking this process of discovery, the work of reconciliation, whereby a son's memories of his father are integrated with an acceptance of who each is, continues beyond death.

After a father dies, for example, the middle-aged son can find himself suddenly cast as the "family elder." This drastic change of status overturns his earliest, internalized images of his father, and forces him once again to revisit separation issues. At the same time, he may need to sort out his relationship to his mother, particularly if she survives his father. If this involves caring for her, certain themes from the past—such as oedipal anxieties concerning physical closeness as well as unresolved anger—may recur and require that they be worked on as well. When the middle-aged son is once again left "alone" with his elderly mother, feelings, impulses, and fantasies that seemed buried long ago may resurface. In the same way that the son experienced the reversal of roles and generations with his aging father, he is called upon to rework old issues and come to new understandings.

The benefits of a healthy father-son relationship have the power to transcend death. If the son is not riddled with deeply rooted ambivalence toward his father, then his grieving process can proceed naturally, along the lines of what Freud described in his classic paper on "Mourning and Melancholia."[11] As Freud explains, if the son is able to be conscious of both his angry, hateful, resentful feelings and his loving, caring, and connected feelings toward his father, he is much more able to integrate them and move on with his life. However, when this healthy mourning or grieving process does not occur, usually because the son cannot own his angry and negative feelings toward a loved father, or when a son so resents his dead father that he can't experience any love or compassion, then the surviving son is trapped in a perpetual state of bereavement. Unable either to mourn fully or to let go of his father (much like my self-denigrating patient, Warren), the son ends up crippled by guilt and self-condemnation. It's as if the deceased, highly critical father simply is incorporated inside the son, who is left to experience these attacks upon himself.

When the father-son relationship has been good enough—or in the cases in which it hasn't but father and son have nonetheless been reconciled—the son is better able to integrate his disappointment toward his father with his love. He can accept that there are hopes that will remain unredeemed and can forgive his father for his failings. In these circumstances, grieving tends to occur more naturally, moving through its phases of sadness and loss, anger, care, gratitude, and letting go.

Joni Mitchell's famous song, "The Circle Game," fittingly chronicles the adventures of a little boy becoming a man who will one day become the father of a little boy himself.[12] This conceptualization of life resonates with many of the world's great religions that also speak about the journey not ending with death, but instead continuing in unexpected and surprising ways.

Just as fathers and sons needed each other as they moved through the earlier stages of their lives—toddlerhood, latency, adolescence, young and maturing adulthood—and were uniquely positioned to offer each other help and guidance neither could find elsewhere, so they are also able to help each other through life's final transitions. This guidance is available until our last moments on earth. Those fathers and sons who meet the challenges of maintaining a close and engaged relationship will more likely feel restored rather than depleted, and will look ahead rather than dwell on what's behind. They will meet new challenges, and discover new possibilities for rejuvenation and restoration, achieving even deeper levels of connection and reconciliation. Near the end of their respective lives, they may both realize that they have attained a mature wisdom that in itself is a singular achievement. This wisdom helps each to see that there are always opportunities to reflect on, recognize, integrate, and appreciate life in its most nuanced and rich variations, to welcome the true circularity of our existence and to fully embrace the fact that though no one person survives death, our legacies do live on.

The death of the patriarch Jacob, movingly described in the Book of Genesis, shows us that Jacob well understood the responsibilities a dying man has to his children. Sensing that the end was near, he summoned his twelve sons to his beside: "Come together," he said, "That I may tell you what is to befall you in days to come." He then proceeded to address each son individually, offering wisdom and advice. When he was done, he said, "I am about to be gathered to my kin. Bury me with my fathers."[13] Often, this promise of continuity is the last and greatest gift from father to son.

EPILOGUE: THE ARC OF LIFE

It is a wise father that knows his own child.

—SHAKESPEARE, *The Merchant of Venice*

Throughout this book, I have asked my readers to reflect on fathers and sons as they journey through the life cycle, from birth to death. Regardless of whether they are in or out of step with each other, they are uniquely positioned to help one another through each of life's major transitions. I believe that when a father and son are able to influence each other in this way, both achieve a deep and lasting understanding of what it means to become a man.

Less explicitly, I have also invited each of you to conceptualize the arc of your own life, to reflect on the stages that we all undergo, and somehow to make sense of how they impact us personally. Writers, philosophers, and great thinkers have tried to answer these questions by proposing various patterns that give meaning to our lives. Shakespeare, for instance, in *As You Like It*, posited man's "seven ages." According to his reckoning, we begin as a crying infant, grow to be a schoolboy, lover, soldier, young man, middle-aged man, and then descend into our dotage, or "second childishness," followed by "mere oblivion." Many psychologists, psychoanalysts, and other social scientists have discussed these phases in less poetic terms, yet few have considered the significance of fathering in the developmental unfolding of a man's life. By adding fathering to the measure of a man, I have elaborated on how an adult male's journey is profoundly affected by the manner in which he embraces fatherhood. Thus, rather than thinking that children *develop* and adults merely *age*, this book stresses the mutual, reciprocal development in the father-son connection. In other words, a son and his father grow and change throughout their lives partly *because of* one another.

Adult development, like child development, isn't relentlessly linear but, instead, a series of advances and retreats. As adults, we expect these regressions in our children, such as the three- or four-year-old who has been toilet-trained yet starts to have accidents as he begins preschool or the teenager who, when told that he can't stay out late, has a temper tantrum. But children aren't the only ones who take two steps forward and one step back. The road to mature adulthood is often roundabout and we all are inclined to regressions and diversions even as we move forward in our lives.

During a man's circuitous journey, he has the opportunity to revisit and reevaluate many cherished notions that he once considered more fixed than they are. As I've discussed in several chapters, even a male's sense of his gender identity is continually being reworked, evoking distinct challenges at varying periods of life. For example, in late adolescence and early adulthood, a young man's sense of his masculinity is often tied to his sexual prowess and ability to endure pain. In his adult years, he is more likely to appraise his manhood in terms of his career success and ability to provide for his family. And finally, in his mid- and later life, his manliness becomes more flexible in the course of his evaluating the success of his fatherliness and generativity. This is the time when his nurturing and feminine sides are more fully integrated into his notion of mature masculinity.

These events don't happen in a vacuum—a man's development influences and is affected by those around him. In this book, I've taken a magnifying glass to one of life's most significant reciprocal relationships: that of a father and son. Nothing about this relationship is static; it changes throughout the lives of both individuals as fathers and sons grow close and pull away, forming alliances and locking horns. Yet through all its permutations and complexities, the relationship remains one of the bedrock relationships of our lives.

CONSTRUCTIVE CHANGE: BREAKING "THE REPETITION COMPULSION"

Nonetheless, this keystone relationship between father and son can go in many directions. As I've detailed, fathers can engage deeply and constructively with their sons, learning to recognize and affirm their uniqueness, and protect, provide, guide, and mentor them to develop as men. But fathers can also neglect, abandon, and abuse their sons, or simply fail to guide them to become effective in the world. What about those boys who don't have the benefit of good enough fathering? Can they also adequately thrive in adulthood and, in turn, become good enough fathers themselves?

The answer is yes. Indeed, even these men can overcome the

ill effects of their fathers' incomplete fathering, particularly with the help of others. Many examples throughout this book delineate how these men, in learning about themselves and their sons, can find ways to enable their immature masculinity to consolidate into a more mature understanding of themselves and others. The most significant benefit of such an understanding is that it gives men the opportunity to avoid repeating, with their own sons, daughters, and wives, some of the damage that may have been done to them as a child. As Euripides said nearly twenty-five hundred years ago, "The gods visit the sins of the fathers upon the children."[1] To break this cycle of what Freud called "the repetition compulsion," a man needs to become more conscious of his relationship to his own father, and in particular, to recognize the ways in which he has unconsciously incorporated disliked traits of his father.[2] This is illustrated by the vignette in chapter 8 where Eric, my thirty-five-year-old patient, courageously faced and took responsibility for his contemptuous behavior with his own son, Mason, just as his father, Russell, had done with him. With requisite insight and awareness, a man won't simply repeat the past, either by unconsciously enacting it or by reflexively doing the opposite of what was done to him.

I too have had to struggle with certain identifications that I made with my father. In turn, I've tried to avoid reenacting with my son some of the interactions that took place between my father and me. Because his mother and oldest sister largely raised him, my father grew up with his share of difficulties in actively dealing with conflict and aggression. When he became a parent, he did as his father had done, and like many men of his generation, left the childrearing primarily to women, in my case to my mother and grandmother (with whom I shared a room during my formative years). As a result, my father wasn't able to help me learn to deal very effectively with my early individuating needs and more aggressive tendencies, but rather acquiesced to my mother in this realm.

In my own efforts to father well, partly as a result of my father's difficulties in asserting himself within the domestic domain, I've had to face my own tendencies to withdraw from familial conflict in order to play out the role of the "good" father. But turning away from potential conflict doesn't help either of my children, let alone my wife. Part of the challenge that I've faced over the years is to force myself continually to reengage when my more avoidant impulses take hold. This necessitates admitting to myself the ways in which I carry inside my own sense of being a "reluctant" father. Consequently, instead of withdrawing from potentially volatile conflict, I try to assert my paternal perspective on my children's needs when required and find successful ways to reestablish the parenting alliance with my wife. This requires that I support her while still recognizing and affirming my son's efforts to forge his own identity.

In addition, it is very important that I, as a father, do what I can to help my wife to champion our son's development. A mother who is able to recognize, support, and affirm her son's maleness—who is *not* threatened by his aggression and separation needs nor herself hateful of men—helps raise sons with fewer internal conflicts in these domains.

For example, how a mother handles her son's attempts to separate from her is important. She needs to contain her own separation anxieties, fears of loss, and envious feelings about her boy's forays into the world of men and the budding father-son relationship. A son who is not supported by his mother during his separation from her will often internalize an antagonism toward both his father and, at times, even his own maleness. This enmity will ultimately impede his developing healthy aggression, mastery, and authority, typically because he incorrectly tends to conclude that his "masculine" aggression represents an attack on women or femininity.

Involved fathers can largely prevent this when these issues surface by teaching their partners about parenting boys and stepping in to normalize their sons' burgeoning masculinity. They can mainly do this by serving as translators, interpreting their sons' behavior so that their wives can understand it and place it within a helpful context. A father who can negotiate this deeper understanding of his son with his spouse strengthens their parenting alliance. Under these favorable circumstances, regardless of the son's age, a son is more likely to experience himself as a good son who is loved by a good mother and good father together. I have observed that sons who carry this triangular sense of worthiness are more able to enter into loving and committed relationships with suitable partners.

In the final analysis, both parents need to support their son's ties to the other parent. If they don't, their son's masculine sense of worth will likely be damaged.

As the psychologist Stephen Ducat writes: ". . . boys who grow up in these circumstances are less destructively envious of mothers and other women, more able to embrace identification with both mothers and fathers, less fearful and disparaging of women and the 'feminine' in themselves, and less inclined to engage in hyper-masculine acting out in adulthood."[3]

A FATHER'S LEGACY

My wife's efforts and my own have paid off. I began this book several years ago, when our daughter left for college. When I first sat down to write this concluding chapter, my wife and I had just returned from taking our eighteen-year-old son to Boston to enter his freshman year in college.

It's hard for a man to imagine, holding his newborn son in his arms, that one day this boy will go off to kindergarten by himself, learn to drive, establish a career, have children of his own, and eventually grow old. Yet our experience as parents is infused with the notion that the closer we hold our children, the more we know that eventually we have to let them go. And if we occasionally forget this essential fact, our children remind us. They wriggle and squirm out of our arms, out of the curfews we try to impose on them, and shut their ears to the sound advice we try to offer them. Exultation and loss are inextricably bound. The simultaneous experience of joy and sadness, as we watch our children grow and leave home, is the very circle of life.

Yet as a father cuddles his baby, or sees him walk out the door on his first date, he isn't only fast-forwarding but back-pedaling. A father's younger self is also in the room watching himself going off to his first school, scoring that winning run, falling in love, gazing upon his firstborn child. Joining him in these scenes is his own father, with whom he continues to be in internal conversation, regardless of whether his father is living or deceased.

With our youngest child gone, our house suddenly began to seem much larger and strangely quieter. Concomitantly, my internal, psychic sense of space also feels wider and less encumbered. I feel both lighter and heavier knowing that my influence on my son is waning forever. My sadness is coupled with an ineffable joy in knowing that my "little boy," now residing more inside me largely as a set of mostly rich and wonderful memories, is emerging as a young man who, like the young woman his sister has become, is someone I will delight in getting to know anew, and with whom I'll form a relationship in the years ahead. We shall soon be two adult men together going through our different stages of life. I can only hope that he too will take pleasure in recognizing and relating to me in ways that he never has before.

Whatever the future may bring, I look forward to the parallel journeys that my children and I began long ago, continuing what I shared with my own father—namely, being together and apart, throughout the mysteries and uncertainties of our respective lives.

Loss and grieving, appreciation and gratitude, disappointment and acceptance—these are all feelings and attitudes that become more nuanced and better assimilated in both father and son's lifelong maturational process. If all goes well enough, each man is likely to emerge in his later years with a sense of mature wisdom that allows both father and son to more fully appreciate the cyclical yet progressive nature of life in the context of authentic, caring connections.

In this way, through his children, a father enhances his link to eternity. Each time a man forges a new connection to his children and each time he lets them go, he bestows an invaluable gift to the next generation. Even after death, the rich, unchanging, intrapsychic legacy of being a father's son lives on. As Philip Roth writes in *Patrimony*, ". . . if not in my books or in my life, at least in my dreams I would live perennially as his little son, with the conscience of a little son, just as he would remain alive there not only as my father but as *the* father, sitting in judgment on whatever I do."[4]

In short, how a man thinks and behaves as a father has enormous ramifications. His attitudes and actions become part of the family chronicle, a story that will be retold and relived countless times, both while he's alive and long thereafter. When these stories are recounted, a shared reality is acknowledged that frequently enables a son to feel closer to his father, and allows a father to experience the prominent position he holds—and will always hold—in his son's life.

INTERGENERATIONAL BONDS

Throughout this book, I have emphasized the importance of the intergenerational continuity of the father-son bond. I know about this bond from inside out. Shortly before my father's death, with his health in decline, my sister and I decided to move him into a nursing home. Though his heart was strong, he was confined to a wheelchair and his speech and cognitive faculties were greatly diminished. He slept most of the time and communicated by making eye contact, smiling, nodding his head, and occasionally grunting. My son, Alex, then six, regularly accompanied me on visits to my father. Though he frequently was bored and ready to leave shortly after arriving, he rarely declined an invitation to visit with his "Papa."

One Saturday, a beautiful Southern California fall afternoon, Alex and I decided to take my father for a walk in his wheelchair outside the grounds. As Alex guided the wheelchair on the residential street, I found myself recalling how my father used to sing to me when I was a boy, typically his favorite Tin Pan Alley standards. When I asked my father if he remembered any of those songs he loved so dearly, he nodded and started to mouth the words to "When the Red Red Robin Comes Bob Bob Bobbin' Along." Alex burst into a smile and said, "I know that one, Papa." He knew it because I'd sung it to him when he was a toddler. Soon, all three of us were singing together. We continued circling the block, giving my father time to teach Alex some "new" songs—"Side by Side," "Tea for Two," and "I Want a Girl (Just Like the Girl that Married Dear Old Dad)," while Alex offered up his rendition of Raffi's "Baby Beluga." The afternoon flew by as we three shamelessly lifted our voices together, with laughter and smiles all around. Arriving back at the home, my dad thanked us. I noticed that Alex had my father's twinkle in his eyes as he kissed his grandfather good-bye. As Alex and I walked home together, I could virtually touch the *joie de vivre* that my father had transmitted to his grandson through me.

A year later, when he turned ninety-six, my father began to fail. I wasn't surprised when, one morning, I received a call from the nursing home that he had passed away. When I arrived at his room, I spent a few minutes with him, noting how peaceful he looked after the taxing last few weeks which he'd spent in and out of the hospital. I felt very relieved. In fact, I had been grieving for the man that I had known for several years. Not surprisingly, my grief was rather like my life with my father—gentle, emotionally unencumbered, and largely conflict-free.

We buried him a few days later and I led the service, reading some of his writings (he took great pride in the letters and poems that he had left with me years ago) and sharing my thoughts on the meaning of his life. Other friends and family joined in at the small graveside service during which my children, my wife, and I had the opportunity to say good-bye to my father.

But of course, as I've made clear throughout this book, I didn't really say good-bye. My father remains with me today, more than a decade later, in my dreams and fleeting thoughts as well as in less effable ways, not the least of which is the spirit in which I embrace fathering and share myself in writing this book. My father's strengths and his failings remain alive with me. And as I reflect on my father, my son, and my own life, I envision an invisible elastic chord that keeps each of us free to move apart yet bound together in countless ways across time and space.

Although my father never had the opportunity to hear his grandson play the saxophone or watch him tear around the bases as his own son once had, I'm sure that both my father and my son knew that they were joined by something rich and valuable that would survive the ravages of aging and the innocence of childhood. Even if it's only as an unconscious memory or feeling, my son carries within him a deep sense of his grandfather and the loving man-to-man connection passed on through the generations. I have no doubt that if afforded the opportunity to be a father himself, Alex will pass on this loving fatherliness to the next generation.

I wrote this book hoping to educate men to father their sons well so that both can continue to develop and grow within the context of a loving relationship. In fact, the educating of fathers has long been a focus of concern. We see this in the Book of Genesis, which, in a certain light, can be thought of as a work dedicated to ushering men into the work of fatherhood so that they may transmit a worthy way of life to their sons and descendants. Think of Abraham and his son Isaac, Isaac and his sons Jacob and Esau, and Jacob with his twelve sons—all wrestling with and learning from each other, living in one another's shadows. From my perspective, however, this education should not focus primarily on teaching techniques or strategies, but instead must offer a process or an approach that subsumes an *appreciation* of a child's otherness, a *capacity* to thoughtfully reflect on oneself, the *courage* to act or choose not to when necessary, and the *willingness* to remain involved and engaged throughout the vicissitudes of an ever-changing, lifelong process.

This fatherly capacity for recognizing his son's uniqueness—whether it occurs early, midway, or later in either's life—also allows men to glimpse the ineffable, indescribable preciousness and fragility of life. The clock of our own mortality begins ticking the day we are born, yet we often begin to hear it more clearly when we become parents. Men become sensitized to "father time," a way of thinking about the past, present, and future in terms of their relationship to their children. Viewing his newborn son for the first time, nurturing this new life, mentoring him, struggling with his efforts to differentiate—in short, becoming intimate with a person who is so much like himself but uniquely different—each new father glimpses his own mortality, and his chance for immortality. "Barring a tragedy," the engaged father says to himself, "my son will outlive me. He is my second chance." In this way, by recognizing and appreciating his son's uniqueness time and again, he forges a bond that will survive space and time, and strengthens his legacy to future generations.

Men don't need to become fathers themselves in order to attain this understanding. However, those men who are fathers have unique opportunities to learn about being a man along with their sons. The contradictions inherent in manhood and brought to life in a man's fatherliness challenge us to stay open and attain a level of comfort with our own ambiguities and those of others. Moreover, fathers who experience parenthood as central to their identity as men are laying the groundwork for their own and their sons' new understanding of masculinity as I've explored it in these pages. Because they aren't defensive or ashamed about being males who provide care for others, they don't need to defend their masculinity so fiercely. They value connection as much as autonomy. They are able to accept vulnerability, weakness, and dependence while simultaneously moving toward strength, authority, and interdependence. In short, they can see masculinity and femininity as a single, fluid continuum along which everyone travels rather than viewing the masculine and feminine as polar, mutually exclusive extremes. In sum, no other facet of a man's existence challenges him more directly to confront the paradoxical nature of his internal life and ultimately achieve the wisdom embraced by Walt Whitman when he declared:

> *Do I contradict myself?*
> *Very well then . . . I contradict myself;*
> *I am large. I contain multitudes.*[5]

NOTES

EPIGRAPH

1. Plato, *Republic*, trans. H. D. Lee (New York: Penguin, 1955), p. 52.

INTRODUCTION

1. The term "forgotten parent" first appeared in the psychoanalytic literature in John Munder Ross's paper entitled "Fathering: A review of some psychoanalytic contributions on paternity," *International Journal of Psychoanalysis*, 60 (1979): 317–28. I subsequently employed the term in an article entitled "Becoming a Father: A psychoanalytic perspective on the forgotten parent," *Psychoanalytic Review*, 73 (1986): 445–68.
2. Although my focus is largely on men in traditional families, the father-son issues that I explore are applicable to all fathers—fathers of adopted children and of stepchildren, late-time fathers, single and surrogate fathers, and fathers in non-traditional relationships such as gay fathers, stay-at-home dads, and fathers serving as primary nurturers. My observations and clinical findings suggest that these core challenges of fathering sons and the reciprocal, lifelong influences upon one another operate across a wide range of familial arrangements. Furthermore, I am not arguing that fathers are more important than mothers in raising sons. Mothers in fact play a cru-

cial role in helping their sons to develop and oftentimes are able to do so quite successfully without co-parenting with a man, as suggested in the writings of the family therapist Olga Silverstein and the clinical psychologist Peggy Drexler—see O. Silverstein and B. Rashbaum, *The Courage to Raise Good Men* (New York: Viking Press, 1994), and P. Drexler, *Raising Boys Without Men* (Emmaus, PA: Rodale Press, 2005).

3. K. D. Pruett, *Fatherneed: Why Fathercare Is as Essential as Mothercare for Your Child* (New York: Free Press, 2000).

4. The interested reader may wish to consult my original published research and writings (listed chronologically): M. J. Diamond, "Becoming a Father: A psychoanalytic perspective on the forgotten parent," *Psychoanalytic Review,* 73 (1986): 445–68; "Creativity. Needs in Becoming a Father," *Journal of Men's Studies,* 1 (1992): 41–45; "Someone to Watch Over Me: The father as the original protector of the mother-infant dyad," *Psychoanalysis and Psychotherapy,* 12 (1995): 89–102; "Boys to Men: The maturing of masculine gender identity through paternal watchful protectiveness," *Gender and Psychoanalysis,* 2 (1997): 443–68; "Fathers with Sons: Psychoanalytic perspectives on 'good enough' fathering throughout the life cycle," *Gender and Psychoanalysis,* 3 (1998): 243–99; "Accessing the Multitude Within: A psychoanalytic perspective on the transformation of masculinity at mid-life," *International Journal of Psychoanalysis,* 85 (2004): 45–64; "The Shaping of Masculinity: Revisioning boys turning away from their mothers to construct male gender identity," *International Journal of Psychoanalysis,* 85 (2004): 359–80; and "Masculinity Unraveled: The roots of male gender identity and the shifting of male ego ideals throughout life," *Journal of the American Psychoanalytic Association,* 54 (2006): 1099–130.

5. This is in no way to suggest that its importance for female readers be neglected, particularly because women can often learn to better understand and appreciate the men in their lives—whether husbands, sons, or fathers. In fact, this book will enable women to develop their understanding of men. It is also my hope that as women learn to guide and support their sons on their journeys, their relationships with all these key people can improve over time. In short, by incorporating these insights, both men and women can

become better parents and partners, and better adult children to their own aging parents.

6. William Wordsworth (1802), "My heart leaps up when I behold," in *English Romantic Poetry*, Vol. I, ed. Harold Bloom (New York: Anchor Books, 1963), p. 302.

CHAPTER 1 · FATHERHOOD ON THE HORIZON

1. Hasdai Ibn Crescas, *The Wisdom of Judaism* (c. 1230), ed. D. Salwak (Novato, CA: New World Library, 1997), p. 102.
2. The developmental psychoanalyst Teresa Benedek coined this term. See T. Benedek, "Fatherhood and Providing," in *Parenthood*, ed. E. J. Anthony and T. Benedek (Boston: Little, Brown, 1970), pp. 167–83.
3. Psychiatrist Martin Greenberg uses the term "engrossment" in his book *The Birth of a Father* (New York: Continuum, 1985). See also the article in which Greenberg first coined the term: M. Greenberg and N. Morris, "Engrossment: The newborn's impact upon the father," *American Journal of Orthopsychiatry*, 44 (1974): 520–31.
4. Kyle Pruett reported this finding reached from his own research in Pruett, *The Nurturing Father* (New York: Warner Books, 1987).
5. Jerrold L. Shapiro, *When Men Are Pregnant: Needs and Concerns of Expectant Fathers* (New York: Delta, 1987).
6. I initially presented these ideas in "Creativity Needs in Becoming a Father," *Journal of Men's Studies*, 1 (1992): 41–45.

CHAPTER 2 · A FATHER IS BORN

1. Sigmund Freud, "Civilization and Its Discontents" (1930) in *The Standard Edition of the Complete Psychological Works of Sigmund Freud* (London: Hogarth Press, 1961, cited hereafter as *SE*), Vol. XXI, pp. 57–145; the quote is on p. 72.
2. Peter Wolson, "Some Reflections on Adaptive Grandiosity in Fatherhood," in *Becoming A Father: Contemporary Social, Developmental, and Clinical Perspective*, ed. J. L. Shapiro, M. J. Diamond, and M. Greenberg (New York: Springer, 1995), pp. 286–92.
3. J. J. Rousseau, *Émile* (1762), trans. A. Bloom (London: Penguin, 1991). In line with this idea, the psychoanalyst Mark O'Connell

recently argued that the disparity in parental preparedness is based on the fact that in contrast to men, women begin to live in their sexual and procreative bodies earlier and more fully. Consequently, they feel their motherhood in a more palpable way and are prepared for parenting much earlier. See M. O'Connell, *The Good Father* (New York: Scribner, 2005).

4. The expression "good enough mother" was first used in Winnicott's 1960 paper "Ego Distortion in Terms of True and False Self," reprinted in D. W. Winnicott's *The Maturational Process and the Facilitating Environment* (New York: International Universities Press, 1965), pp. 140–52. I employ the term "good enough" father and discuss its meaning in "Fathers with Sons: Psychoanalytic perspectives on 'good enough' fathering throughout the life cycle."

5. Child psychoanalyst James Herzog coined the term "father hunger." Two of his writings are particularly germane: J. M. Herzog, "On Father Hunger: The Father's Role in the Modulation of Aggressive Drive and Fantasy," in *Father and Child,* ed. S. H. Cath, A. R. Gurwitt, and J. M. Ross (Boston: Little, Brown, 1982), pp. 163–74, and J. M. Herzog, *Father Hunger* (Hillsdale, NJ: Analytic Press, 2001). Developmental researchers Michael Lamb and Rob Palkovitz have provided comprehensive reviews of the vast literature pertaining to a father's impact on his sons (and daughters). The evidence indicates a strong consensus that the absence of an involved, emotionally invested father has deleterious consequences on his son. In general, the effects are most pronounced in the areas of a son's self-control, self-esteem, cognitive competence, emotional self-regulation, sense of masculinity, empathy, school performance, social skills, and overall well-being. See M. E. Lamb, "Fathers and Child Development: An Integrative Overview," in *The Role of the Father in Child Development,* ed. M. E. Lamb (New York: John Wiley, 1981), pp. 1–70; M. E. Lamb, "Fathers and Child Development: An Introductory Overview," in *The Role of the Father in Child Development,* 3rd edn., ed. M. E. Lamb (New York: John Wiley, 1997), pp. 1–18; and R. Palkovitz, "Involved Fathering and Child Development: Advancing Our Understanding of Good Fathering," in *Handbook of Father Involvement: Multidisciplinary Perspectives,* ed. C. S. Tamis-LeMonda and N. Cabrera (Mahwah, NJ: Erlbaum, 2002), pp. 119–40.

6. I introduced the term "watchful protector" in "Boys to Men: The

maturing of masculine gender identity through paternal watchful protectiveness."

7. David Gilmore, *Manhood in the Making: Cultural Concepts of Masculinity* (New Haven, CT: Yale University Press, 1990), p. 230.

8. Jeffrey Masson, *The Emperor's Embrace: Reflections on Animal Families and Fatherhood* (New York: Pocket Books, 1999), pp. 199–200.

9. This idea has been greatly elaborated by John Bowlby, particularly in *A Secure Base* (New York: Basic Books, 1988).

10. Donald W. Winnicott introduced this term and eloquently discussed its importance. See in particular D. W. Winnicott, "Primary Maternal Preoccupation," in D. W. Winnicott's *Collected Papers: Through Pediatrics to Psycho-Analysis* (New York: Basic Books, 1958), pp. 300–05.

11. I discuss this evidence in my monograph "Fathers with Sons: Psychoanalytic perspectives on 'good enough' fathering throughout the life cycle"; see pp. 252–53 for a discussion of these studies. In addition, James Herzog has written extensively about the impact of such a "deficit" on male children (see note 5 above).

12. Benedek, "Fatherhood and Providing," in *Parenthood*, pp. 167–83.

13. See Bowlby, *A Secure Base*.

14. After three months or so, as James Herzog suggests, the wife often needs her husband to maintain the sexual component of "spousing and caregiving," particularly in the face of a mother's wishes that her husband remain "the nonsexual man who can entertain the child" (p. 66)—see J. Herzog, "What Fathers Do and How They Do It," in *What Do Mothers Want?*, ed. S. F. Brown (Hillsdale, NJ: Analytic Press, 2005), pp. 55–68.

15. Psychoanalysts maintain that it is extremely important for a child to be able to represent his parents—the parental couple—together in order to create what Kleinian analyst Ronald Britton terms "triangular space" and what James Herzog calls "triadic reality." This unconscious internal representation that links the mother with the father sets the stage for the boy's experience of being jointly regarded by his parents (rather than individually appropriated by either for their own needs) and serves as a prerequisite for his healthy negotiation of the subsequent oedipal phase. See R. Britton, "The Missing Link: Parental Sexuality in the Oedipus Conflict," in *The Oedipus Con-*

flict Today, ed. J. Steiner (London: Karnac Books, 1989), pp. 83–102; and J. M. Herzog, "Triadic Reality and the Capacity to Love," Psychoanalytic Quarterly, 74 (2005): 1029–52.

CHAPTER 3 · FATHERS INTRODUCING TODDLERS TO THE WORLD

1. Proverb quoted in Gail Collins, "A New Look at Life with Father," New York Times Magazine, June 17, 1979.
2. Child psychiatrist and psychoanalyst Stanley Greenspan introduced the term "second other" in referring to the father as the distinct other figure apart from the child's most significant other, that is, mother; see S. I. Greenspan, " 'The Second Other': The Role of the Father in Early Personality Formation and the Dyadic-Phallic Phase of Development," in Father and Child, ed. S. H. Cath, A. R. Gurwitt, and J. M. Ross (Boston: Little Brown, 1982), pp. 123–38. Psychoanalyst Jessica Benjamin subsequently developed the idea that the father "represents 'difference'" and that the second other invariably carries a paternal quality; see J. Benjamin, Like Subjects, Like Objects (New Haven: Yale University Press, 1995, p. 62).
3. D. J. Siegel, The Developing Mind: Toward a Neurobiology of Interpersonal Experience (New York: Guilford Press, 1999); see also D. J. Siegel, Mindset (New York: Bantam Books, 2006).
4. James Herzog used these terms to describe the preferred parent-child interactive play modes of fathers and mothers respectively; see Herzog, Father Hunger.
5. The Swiss psychologist Jean Piaget introduced the term "object permanence" in J. Piaget, The Construction of Reality in the Child (1937; New York: Bantam Books, 1954). The ego psychologist Heinz Hartmann brought the idea of object constancy into mainstream psychoanalysis. Hartmann declared that object constancy was achieved when the relation to a loved one endures and remains stable regardless of the state of the child's needs—see Heinz Hartmann, "The Mutual Influences in the Development of the Ego and Id," in Essays in Ego Psychology, ed. Hartmann (1952; New York: International Universities Press, 1964), pp. 155–82.
6. Allan Schore, Affect Regulation and the Origin of the Self: The Neurobiology of Emotional Development (Hillsdale, NJ: Erlbaum, 1994);

see also Allan Schore, *Affect Disregulation and Disorders of the Self* (New York: W. W. Norton, 2003).

7. Sadly, many little girls are encouraged to be "objects" of someone else's desire without feeling entitled to wanting anything for themselves. As Jessica Benjamin maintains in *The Bonds of Love* (New York: Pantheon Books, 1988, pp. 85–132), this can have lasting implications for female development and eventually for a woman's sense of achievement and ambition. Though not the focus of this book, fathers likewise play a crucial role in their daughters' ability to attain a healthy sense of desire and subjectivity.

CHAPTER 4 · GUIDING BOYS TOWARD THE WORLD OF MEN

1. Tanakh, *The Holy Scriptures*, Proverbs 22:6 (Philadelphia: Jewish Publication Society), p. 1320.

2. See, for example, the following articles: R. Greenson, "Disidentifying from Mother: Its special importance for the boy," *International Journal of Psychoanalysis*, 49 (1968): 370–74; R. J. Stoller, *Sex and Gender*. Vol. I: *The Development of Masculinity and Femininity* (London: Hogarth Press, 1968); I. Fast, "Aspects of Early Gender Development: Toward a reformulation," *Psychoanalytic Psychology*, 7 (Suppl.) (1990): 105–17; S. D. Axelrod, "Developmental Pathways to Masculinity: A reconsideration of Greenson's 'Disidentifying from Mother,'" *Issues in Psychoanalytic Psychology*, 19 (1997): 101–15; W. S. Pollack, *Real Boys: Rescuing Our Sons from the Myths of Boyhood* (New York: Random House, 1998); and Diamond, "The Shaping of Masculinity: Revisioning boys turning away from their mothers to construct male gender identity."

3. A number of psychoanalysts contend that a father's active involvement during the boy's subsequent latency years is required for the healthy development of these pre-oedipal and oedipal phallic strivings. See, for example, R. Edgcumbe and M. Burgner, "The Phallic-Narcissistic Phase," *Psychoanalytic Study of the Child*, 30 (1975): 161–80, and L. J. Schalin, "Phallic Integration and Male Identity Development: Aspects of the importance of the father relation to boys in the latency period," *Scandinavian Psychoanalytic Review*, 6 (1983): 21–42.

4. Developmental psychologist Eleanor Maccoby documented the

many ways in which boys, from the time they are very young, learn that cross-gender behavior is taboo. In contrast, girls by ages six or seven sense that their gender remains stable and intact throughout their lives. They know they'll remain girls regardless of how often they manifest cross-gender attitudes and behavior—see E. E. Maccoby, *The Two Sexes: Growing Apart, Coming Together* (Cambridge, MA: Harvard University Press, 1998), and also E. E. Maccoby and C. Jacklin, *The Psychology of Sex Differences*, Vol. 1 (Palo Alto, CA: Stanford University Press, 1976).

5. Both the Finnish psychoanalyst Vesa Manninen and the psychologist/psychoanalyst Stephen Ducat have offered particularly evocative and illuminating discussions of the seductive power of phallicism. See V. Manninen, "The Ultimate Masculine Striving: Reflexions on the psychology of two polar explorers," *Scandinavian Psychoanalytic Review*, 15 (1992): 1–26; V. Manninen, "For the Sake of Eternity: On the narcissism of fatherhood and the father-son relationship," *Scandinavian Psychoanalytic Review*, 16 (1993): 35–46; and S. J. Ducat, *The Wimp Factor: Gender Gaps, Holy Wars, and the Politics of Anxious Masculinity* (Boston: Beacon Press, 2004). In addition, another Finnish analyst, Lars-Johan Schalin, has distinguished the healthy, adaptive nature of phallicism from the pathologically defensive, especially by emphasizing the bodily component in the desire to penetrate—see Schalin, "On Phallicism: Developmental aspects, neutralization, sublimation and defensive phallicism," *Scandinavian Psychoanalytic Review*, 12 (1989): 38–57.

6. Psychoanalyst Steven Krugman refers to this transition as a "shifting of emphasis" rather than a "precarious leap"—see S. Krugman, "Male Development and the Transformation of Shame," in *The New Psychology of Men*, ed. R. F. Levant and W. S. Pollack (New York: Basic Books, 1995), pp. 91–126 (quote on p. 109).

7. See especially J. M. Ross, "Oedipus Revisited: Laius and the 'Laius Complex,'" *Psychoanalytic Study of the Child*, 37 (1982): 169–200.

8. Pat Conroy, *The Great Santini* (New York: Houghton Mifflin, 1976).

9. See S. Osherson, *Finding Our Fathers* (New York: Free Press, 1986).

CHAPTER 5 · ENCOURAGING MASTERY, COMPETENCE, AND PRIDE IN MIDDLE CHILDHOOD

1. David Crosby, Stephen Stills, Graham Nash, and Neil Young, "Teach Your Children," *Déjà vu*, Atlantic Records, 1970.

2. Sigmund Freud, "Three Essays on the Theory of Sexuality" (1905), in *SE*, Vol. VII, pp. 123–243; see also S. Freud, "The Dissolution of the Oedipus Complex" (1924), in Vol. XIX, pp. 171–79.

3. See Dan Kindlon and Michael Thompson, *Raising Cain: Protecting the Emotional Life of Boys* (New York: Ballantine Books, 1999). In addition, psychologist Susan Bernadette-Shapiro and her colleagues found that the development of empathy in school-aged boys was directly related to the amount of time spent with their fathers—see S. Bernadette-Shapiro, D. Ehrensaft, and J. L. Shapiro, "Father Participation in Childcare and the Development of Empathy in Sons: An empirical study," *Family Therapy*, 23 (1996): 77–93. Consistent with my own thesis, these authors hypothesized that as a result of the father's active participation, the boy develops a more secure masculine identification and consequently has less need to defend against the "feminine" aspects of himself, such as empathy (see esp. p. 88).

4. See Pollack, *Real Boys: Rescuing Our Sons from the Myths of Boyhood*.

5. See Herzog, *Father Hunger*.

6. In Erik H. Erikson, *Identity, Youth, and Crisis* (New York: W. W. Norton, 1968).

7. This process of "phallic integration" partially depends on the active involvement of an admired father. By identifying with his actual and realistic father, the boy's ego ideal loses its phallic-grandiose traits and makes room for human weaknesses—see Schalin, "Phallic Integration and Male Identity Development."

8. Anonymous, "A tiny poem to my Dad," in P. Blos, *Son and Father: Before and Beyond the Oedipus Complex* (New York: Free Press, 1985), p. 55.

9. J. Rumi, *Open Secret: Versions of Rumi*, trans. J. Moyne and C. Barks (Putney, VT: Threshold Books, 1984), p. 15.

10. See Carol Gilligan, *In a Different Voice* (Cambridge, MA: Harvard University Press, 1982).

11. C. G. Jung, *Symbols of Transformation, Collected Works of Carl G.*

Jung, Vol. V, trans. R. F. C. Hull (Princeton, NJ: Princeton University Press, 1956), p. 261; J. Lacan, *Écrits: A Selection*, trans. A. Sheridan (1966; New York: W. W. Norton, 1977).

12. See Jean Piaget, *The Origins of Intelligence in Children* (1936; New York: W. W. Norton, 1963).

CHAPTER 6 · FROM HERO TO FALLEN HERO

1. J. D. Salinger, *The Catcher in the Rye* (New York: Bantam Books, 1945), p. 214.
2. P. Blos, "The Second Individuation Process of Adolescence," *Psychoanalytic Study of the Child*, 22 (1967): 162–87.
3. This phrase was used by the psychoanalyst Hans Loewald; see H. Loewald, "The Waning of the Oedipus Complex," *Journal of the American Psychoanalytic Association*, 27 (1979): 751–75 (the expression is introduced on p. 757).
4. See the research findings reported in D. Offer, *The Psychological World of the Teenager: A Study of Normal Adolescent Boys* (New York: Basic Books, 1969), and D. Offer, "Adolescent Development: A Normative Perspective," in *The Course of Life*. Vol. II. *Latency, Adolescence and Youth*, ed. S. I. Greenspan and G. H. Pollock (Washington, D.C.: National Institute of Mental Health, 1980), pp. 357–72.
5. Peter Blos elaborated some of these ideas, albeit without focusing primarily on the father's role, in his seminal 1967 paper (see note 2 above), and subsequently in *Son and Father: Before and Beyond the Oedipus Complex*.
6. Raymond Carver, "Bicycles, Muscles, Cigarettes," in *Where I'm Calling From: Selected Stories* (New York: Vintage Books, 1986), pp. 21–33; the quoted passage is on pp. 32–33.
7. Judith Viorst, *Necessary Losses* (New York: Ballantine Books, 1986), pp. 159, 167.

CHAPTER 7 · COACHING FROM THE SIDELINES

1. Antoine de Saint-Exupéry, *Wind, Sand, and Stars* (1939), trans. L. Galantière (New York: Harcourt, Brace & World, 1967).

2. See Gail Sheehy, *New Passages: Mapping Your Life Across Time* (New York: Ballantine Books, 1995).

3. Calvin Colarusso, a developmentally oriented psychoanalyst, has formulated broad definitions for the three essential individuation processes that occur during adulthood (following the first and second individuations of childhood and adolescence, respectively). See C. A. Colarusso, "The Third Individuation: The effect of biological parenthood on separation-individuation processes in adulthood," *Psychoanalytic Study of the Child,* 45 (1990): 170–94; C. A. Colarusso, Separation-Individuation Processes in Middle Adulthood: The Fourth Individuation," in *The Seasons of Life: Separation-Individuation Perspectives,* ed. S. Akhtar and S. Kramer (Northvale, NJ: Aronson, 1997), pp. 73–94; and C. A. Colarusso, "Separation-Individuation Phenomena in Adulthood: General concepts and the fifth individuation," *Journal of the American Psychoanalytic Association,* 48 (2000): 1467–89.

4. See D. J. Levinson et al., *The Seasons of a Man's Life* (New York: Alfred A. Knopf, 1978).

5. L. F. Baum, *The Wonderful Wizard of Oz* (1900; New York: Dover Books, 1970).

6. Viorst, *Necessary Losses*, p. 234.

7. Sheehy, *New Passages: Mapping Your Life Across Time*, p. 52.

8. See Erik H. Erikson, *Children and Society*, 2nd edn. (New York: W. W. Norton, 1963).

9. Phil Cousineau, "For My Father Who Never Made It to Paris," in Cousineau's *The Blue Museum: Poems* (San Francisco, CA: Sisyphus Press, 2005), pp. 60–61.

10. Sam Osherson, *Finding Our Fathers*, p. 43.

CHAPTER 8 · MAN TO MAN

1. Yiddish proverb in *The Wisdom of Judaism*, ed. D. Salwak p. 101.

2. See Levinson et al., *The Seasons of a Man's Life*.

3. In Erikson, *Childhood and Society*.

4. Stanley H. Cath, "Grandfatherhood, A Timely Transition: The Last Relationship," in *The Course of Life, Vol.VII: Completing the Journey*, ed. G. H. Pollock and S. I. Greenspan (Madison, CT: International Universities Press, 1998), pp. 87–101.

5. E. H. Erikson, J. M. Erikson, and H. Q. Kivnick, *Vital Involvement in Old Age* (New York: W. W. Norton, 1986).

6. Roger L. Gould, "Transformation Tasks in Adulthood," in *The Course of Life, Vol. VI: Late Adulthood*, ed. G. H. Pollock and S. I. Greenspan (Madison, CT: International Universities Press, 1993), pp. 23–68 (the quote is on p. 25).

7. I develop these themes in my article "Accessing the Multitude Within: A psychoanalytic perspective on the transformation of masculinity at mid-life." For further discussion of these important mid-life issues for men, see E. Jacques, "Death and the Mid-life Crisis," *International Journal of Psychoanalysis*, 46 (1965): 502–14; *The Middle Years: New Psychoanalytic Perspectives*, ed. J. M. Oldham and R. S. Liebert (New Haven, CT: Yale University Press, 1989); G. H. Pollock and S. I. Greenspan, *The Course of Life, Vol. VI: Late Adulthood*; and C. A. Colarusso, "The Development of Time Sense in Middle Adulthood," *Psychoanalytic Quarterly*, 68 (1999): 52–83.

8. Levinson and his colleagues observed that most men were presented with these distinct challenges during this time of life—Levinson et al., *The Seasons of a Man's Life*.

9. Though it is far afield from the focus of this book, "transference" in psychoanalytic therapy or psychoanalysis refers to the displacement of feelings and ideas from previous significant figures in the patient's life, or the projections of the patient's state of mind, onto the therapist or analyst. Transference is an especially formidable vehicle for working psychoanalytically with significant "failures" in fathering (or mothering) in that it provides an opportunity to resolve or manage conflicts and developmental arrests dating from infancy and childhood. A therapist who is trained in dealing with the patient's transferences is able to provide a uniquely effective tool for working through the deeper, often more unconscious issues that result from inadequate parenting. This is not "reparenting," but rather psychological work, which enables the patient to come to know himself in a different way, and, in turn, make use of his analyst-therapist's skillful insights to internalize a different way of experiencing himself.

10. Bernice L. Neugarten, "Adult Personality: Toward a Psychology of the Life Cycle," in *Middle Age and Aging*, ed. Neugarten (Chicago: University of Chicago Press, 1968), pp. 137–47 (the quote is on p. 141).

CHAPTER 9 · REVERSING ROLES IN LATER LIFE

1. Walt Whitman, "Song of Myself," in *Leaves of Grass* (1855; New York: Penguin, 1986), p. 40.

2. I incorporate the conclusions of many prominent psychologists and psychoanalysts studying male later-life development. These scholars overwhelmingly agree about the tasks, challenges, and intrapsychic issues that occur for men during middle and late adulthood as elaborated in my article "Accessing the Multitude Within." In addition, the following writings are especially pertinent: C. G. Jung, "The Development of Personality," in *Collected Works*, Vol. XVII (1934; Princeton, NJ: Princeton University Press, 1954), pp. 167–86; E. Jacques, "Death and the Mid-life Crisis"; Levinson et al., *The Seasons of a Man's Life*; C. A. Colarusso, "Separation-Individuation Phenomena in Adulthood: General concepts and the fifth individuation"; and S. D. Axelrod, *Work and the Evolving Self* (Hillsdale, NJ: Analytic Press, 1999).

3. Diamond, "Accessing the Multitude Within," p. 59.

4. See M. R. Lansky, *Fathers Who Fail* (Hillsdale, NJ: Analytic Press, 1992).

5. See C. A. Colarusso, "Traversing Young Adulthood: The male journey from 20 to 40," *Psychoanalytic Inquiry*, 15 (1995): 75–91.

6. See B. L. Neugarten and Associates, *Personality in Middle and Late Life* (New York: Atherton Press, 1964).

7. See Erik H. Erikson, *The Life Cycle Completed* (New York: W. W. Norton, 1982).

8. Ewald W. Busse, "Old Age," in *The Course of Life, Vol. VII: Completing the Journey*, ed. G. H. Pollock and S. I. Greenspan, pp. 1–41.

9. David Gutmann, "Developmental Issues in the Masculine Mid-life Crisis," *Journal of Geriatric Psychiatry*, 9 (1976): 41–61.

10. V. Manninen, "For the Sake of Eternity: On the narcissism of fatherhood and the father-son relationship" (quote on p. 45).

11. Sigmund Freud, "Mourning and Melancholia" (1917), in *SE*, Vol. XIV, pp. 237–58.

12. Joni Mitchell, "The Circle Game," *Ladies of the Canyon*, Reprise Records, 1970.

13. Tanakh, *The Holy Scriptures*, pp. 79, 82.

EPILOGUE: THE ARC OF LIFE

1. This quotation is attributed to Euripides from his play *Phrixus*, of which only fragments exist.

2. The compulsion to repeat refers to an individual's replication of distressing, even painful situations during the course of life without consciously recognizing one's own participation in bringing these about. There is little or no relating of the current incident to past experiences. Freud observed that such repetition in action (including dreams) substitutes for verbal recollection of forgotten memories and consequently is a way of remembering. Other analysts have argued that this "return of the repressed" serves an important ego function, which helps the individual to regulate and master what remains unconscious and unresolved. See Freud, "Beyond the Pleasure Principle" (1920), in *SE*, Vol. XVIII, pp. 7–64. Freud first mentioned this compulsion in "Remembering, Repeating and Working Through" (1914), in Vol. XII, pp. 145–56. See also E. Bibring, "The Conception of the Repetition Compulsion," *Psychoanalytic Quarterly*, 12 (1940): 486–519, and H. W. Loewald, "Some Conclusions on Repetition and Repetition Compulsion," *International Journal of Psychoanalysis*, 52 (1971): 59–65.

3. Ducat, *The Wimp Factor: Gender Gaps, Holy Wars, and the Politics of Anxious Masculinity*, p. 58.

4. Philip Roth, *Patrimony* (New York: Simon & Schuster, 1991), pp. 237–38.

5. Whitman, "Song of Myself," in *Leaves of Grass*, p. 85.

PERMISSIONS

Page 31: *The Emperor's Embrace: Reflections on Animal Families and Fatherhood.* Copyright © 1999 by Jeffery Masson. Reprinted with the permission of the Elaine Markson Literary Agency.

Page 88: "Teach Your Children" by Graham Nash. Copyright © 1970 Nash Notes. All rights administered by Sony/ATV Music Publishing, 8 Music Square West, Nashville, TN 37203. All rights reserved. Used by permission.

Page 97: "A tiny poem to my Dad" by Anonymous, from *Son and Father: Before and Beyond the Oedipus Complex* by Peter Blos. Copyright © 1985 by Peter Blos. All rights reserved. Reprinted with the permission of The Free Press, a Division of Simon & Schuster Adult Publishing Group.

Page 99: *Open Secret: Versions of Rumi* translated by John Moyne and Coleman Barks. Originally published by Threshold Books.

Page 129: "Bicycles, Muscles, Cigarettes" by Raymond Carver, from *Where I'm Calling From: Selected Stories*. Reprinted with the permission of Random House, Inc.

Page 150: "For My Father Who Never Made It to Paris" by Phil Cousineau, from *The Blue Museum: Poems*, Sisyphus Press, 2005. Used by permission of the author.

Page 203: *Patrimony* by Philip Roth. Copyright © 1991 by Philip Roth. Reprinted with the permission of Simon & Schuster Adult Publishing Group.

INDEX